BRANCH LINES
OF THE CHESTER
&
HOLYHEAD RAILWAY

BRANCH LINES OF THE CHESTER & HOLYHEAD RAILWAY

A NEW HISTORY

PHILIP M. LLOYD

AN IMPRINT OF PEN & SWORD BOOKS LTD.
YORKSHIRE – PHILADELPHIA

First published in Great Britain in 2025 by
Pen and Sword Transport
An imprint of
Pen & Sword Books Ltd.
Yorkshire – Philadelphia

Copyright © Philip M. Lloyd, 2025

ISBN 978 1 39904 352 6

The right of Philip M. Lloyd to be identified as Author of this work has been asserted by him in accordance with the Copyright, Designs and Patents Act 1988.

A CIP catalogue record for this book is available from the British Library.

All rights reserved. No part of this book may be reproduced or transmitted in any form or by any means, electronic or mechanical including photocopying, recording or by any information storage and retrieval system, without permission from the Publisher in writing.

Typeset in Times New Roman 12/14.5
by SJmagic DESIGN SERVICES, India.
Printed and bound in India by Replika Press Pvt. Ltd.

Pen & Sword Books Ltd. incorporates the imprints of Pen & Sword Books: After the Battle, Archaeology, Atlas, Aviation, Battleground, Discovery, Family History, History, Maritime, Military, Politics, Select, Transport, True Crime, Fiction, Frontline Books, Leo Cooper, Praetorian Press, Seaforth Publishing, Wharncliffe and White Owl.

For a complete list of Pen & Sword titles please contact

PEN & SWORD BOOKS LIMITED
George House, Beevor Street, Off Pontefract Road, Hoyle Mill, Barnsley,
South Yorkshire, England, S71 1HN.
E-mail: enquiries@pen-and-sword.co.uk
Website: www.pen-and-sword.co.uk

or
PEN AND SWORD BOOKS
1950 Lawrence Rd, Havertown, PA 19083, USA
E-mail: uspen-and-sword@casematepublishers.com
Website: www.penandswordbooks.com

Contents

Preface and Acknowledgements 6

About the Author 8

Author's note 9

Chapter 1   The London and North Western Railway and branch line development in North Wales..10

Chapter 2   The Lines to Denbigh and the struggle for a third force in Welsh railways c1850-1880 23

Chapter 3   LNWR Flintshire and Denbighshire branches in action 1858-1923 48

Chapter 4   The Eastern Slate District 82

Chapter 5   The Western Slate District and Anglesey 111

Chapter 6   The Decline of the North Wales Branch Lines 160

Chapter 7   LNWR branch lines in North Wales: An Overview 193

Colour Picture Gallery 201

Appendix: London and North Western Railway Branch lines in North Wales 217

Bibliography 221

Newspapers 223

Index 225

Preface and Acknowledgements

This history of branch line development in north Wales is a companion volume to *The Chester and Holyhead Railway: A New History* published by Pen and Sword in 2021. The histories of the main line and its branches are connected but the story behind the latter is different. While the Chester and Holyhead Railway (CHR) began as a core item in government policy towards Ireland and was lucrative for the London and North Western Railway (LNWR), its branch lines were of less interest to the company that ran them and served little strategic purpose either nationally or regionally. Apart from the Llandudno to Blaenau Ffestiniog line, the network no longer exists and in many places has left little trace that it ever existed. But exist it did, and its creation, use and demise were sources of strong feelings for over a century. It is that story this book recounts. The book does not include much technical detail about engines, rolling stock and infrastructure, which I include only where they relate to the wider social, economic, and political significance of the branch lines. An appendix supplies detail about all the stations and an incident relating to each if there is one in the text.

I have organised the book by district for the period up to 1923, working from east to west. Each of these district chapters details the creation and building of the railway and examines some operational accidents and incidents. I cover the rapid decline and fall of the branches in a single chapter for the four most northerly counties of north Wales as they were before the 1974 local government reorganisation.

I appreciate the help I have received from the following people and organisations, especially in my effort to supply a photograph for most stations or station locations on the branch network. John Alsop was generous in giving access to his collection. Stephen Rowson was particularly helpful in searching out relevant photographs from the Welsh Railways Research Circle (WRRC) archive (https://www.wrrc.org.uk), as were Mike Musson of the London and North Western Railway Society (https://lnwrs.org.uk/), Peter Waller of the Online Transport Archive (http://www.onlinetransportarchive.org) and David Bird of the Railway Correspondence and Travel Society (https://rcts.org.uk). Richard Ellis-Hobbs supplied pictures from his father's excellent collection. The Geograph resource (https://www.geograph.

org.uk) of photographs that are free to copy under Creative Commons Licence was useful. Michael Stewart was helpful in supplying images of tickets issued on the network. I also express my thanks to Janet Brookes and John Scott-Morgan of Pen & Sword Publishers for their support during personally challenging times for me while writing the book. My wife Ceri was most supportive and spent time helping me to find locations and discussing the development and decline of the railway network in north Wales.

About the Author

Phil Lloyd was born in Stockport and has lived in the north-west of England all his life, apart from a first degree in history and politics at York from 1971. He gained an MA (Econ) and a social work qualification at Manchester University in 1978 and worked as a probation officer until 1998. He led Youth Offending Teams in Manchester and Cheshire before managing in social care in Cheshire. He retired from his post as a director in Cheshire East in 2011 and completed a doctorate in Railway Studies at York in 2017. He now lives in Merseyside with his wife Ceri and spends a lot of time in north Wales.

Author's note

I use lower case for 'north' in north Wales, though it is often 'North' in quoted text. This is now the preferred approach in many publications and supports the notion of Wales as a single entity. Spelling of Welsh placenames has changed on the railway system, and I have tried to use the spelling that was in use at the time when talking about a particular station but mostly use current Welsh spelling when talking about the place, as in 'The station in Caernarfon was spelt as Carnarvon and later Caernarvon'. I am sure that I have not achieved complete accuracy on this point, and I am responsible for all errors on this and other aspects of the book. Where a monetary value is mentioned, I have updated it using the Bank of England inflation calculator, www.bankofengland.co.uk/monetary-policy/inflation/inflation-calculator. This tends to understate the current purchasing power but is used to give a rough comparison.

I have made every effort to find and acknowledge the copyright holder of all photographs and believe that I have done so. However, if I have made an error, please contact me through the publisher.

Chapter 1

The London and North Western Railway and branch line development in North Wales

The leviathan of railway companies ... which exercised a huge and unjust monopoly, and lived upon litigation, selfishly and constantly oppressing the smaller companies.

House of Commons debate, 27 May 1850

This book examines the branch lines in north Wales the LNWR worked, particularly those west of Mold. The branches connected to the CHR were mostly developed, acquired or operated by the LNWR to protect traffic on the main coastal route. The lines did not flow from a regional economic or social motive and for that reason they were not particularly profitable, if they were profitable at all. Readers of the companion volume will know that I argue the government supported the CHR to give more rapid access to Ireland, an aim largely unrelated to the needs of north Wales. Tourism did flow from the CHR and, to a lesser extent, its branches, but the CHR was essentially a political railway that only later became a profitable tourist route for the LNWR. One consequence of this relationship between the LNWR and the region was a persistent tension between the company and local populace and businesses.

Even before the completion of its main line in 1850, the CHR was alert to the dangers of competition in north Wales, especially from the Great Western Railway (GWR). The construction of the CHR began in March 1845, and by September the company announced its intention to build lines along most of the potential routes to the north Wales coast that threatened to create a rival port to Holyhead and access the lucrative Irish traffic:

The Directors of the [CHR] inform the shareholders, that, in accordance with the intimation already made to them, surveys are in progress ... to enable the Company to apply to Parliament in the next session for powers to construct a branch line into the Mold district; and the Directors further announce that their engineers are preparing surveys of branch lines from Rhyl along the Vale of Clwyd to Denbigh, Ruthin, and from Conway along the Conway Valley. By order, GEORGE KING, Secretary.

As the CHR was simultaneously arguing that it could not make enough money from its main line, and was asking government for more concessions on the postal contract, why did it extend its network? By the 1850s it was clear that branch lines were often expensive luxuries, especially when built to main line standards. The 1839 Irish Railway Commission report exposed how engineers, parliamentarians, lawyers, and landowners exploited railway development for profit, even with schemes that had little or no prospect of supplying a return on capital. The commission criticised the approach to railway building that treated every scheme separately with little notion of an overall system, suggesting it served profiteers and not the public.

Edmund Sharpe, a philanthropist, and church builder, who moved to Llanrwst around 1856, applied the logic of the Irish Railway Commission in a lengthy letter to Lord Stanley on the economics of branch lines. He was blunt in his assessment of the practices adopted by railway companies:

> It is not to be supposed, that those who had profited so largely by the construction of the Main Line were unwilling to promote the Branch; the officials of the parent trunk were generally the sponsors of the offshoot; and in this way numerous Branch lines, designed after the model of the original standard, were brought before the public, and carried into execution. Of these minor projects it may, with safety, be affirmed, that few have proved to be other than unprofitable undertakings, and the greater part of them absolutely disastrous to the shareholders, or to the unfortunate parent company which was induced to originate or adopt them; and the lamentable error committed by the Boards of the older Railway Companies, in the purchase and construction of these Branch Railways, is recognized as one of the principal causes of the subsequent decline in the value of Railway property.

Sharpe's solution was to have three levels of branch railway; the first built to main line standards, the second designated a first-class tramway run with steam traction, the third a second-class tramway with horse-drawn traffic. His arguments were consistent with those of the Irish Railway Commission – he wanted to remove the need for legislation, allow freedom to adopt different gauges, build branch lines and stations to lower standards and allow steeper gradients.

Sharpe gave an example of where his scheme would be most effective, a line from Llanrwst to the CHR at Conwy built along the west bank of the river. He suggested a first-class tramway from Conwy to Llanrwst and a second-class tramway thence to Betws-y-Coed. He argued that a narrower gauge enabled easier access to quarries and reduced cost as it needed fewer bridges and other works compared to a first-class branch line on the east side of the river. That was in 1857. We shall see how far he was able to apply his principles and avoid the financial temptations of conventional railway building that he had denounced.

Sharpe was an intelligent, talented, and well-meaning man with a strong record of achievement. His mistake was to apply a logic to the construction of railways that assumed companies built them primarily for the benefit of the public. He therefore missed the application of a different logic, that of competition and of excluding rival companies from potentially fruitful opportunities. North Wales supplied a good example of building or acquiring strategic railway lines for no other reason than stifling competition. The LNWR clearly remained nervous about the GWR, even after the defeat of the latter's proposed railway from Worcester to Porth Dinllaen in 1846 and it regarded most of north Wales as an area from which to exclude the GWR, as seen by the published plans of the CHR noted above. That approach reflected the wishes of its effective owner, the LNWR.

According to the GWR secretary, giving evidence to a select committee in 1853 about this period, the LNWR was keen to sustain its own monopoly and prevent any other company from challenging them. Map 1 below shows the potential directions from which competition in north Wales might come.

There were four parts to establishing the LNWR monopoly of railway traffic in north Wales. In the first phase from 1845-60, the LNWR and GWR struggled for ownership of important lines that accessed north Wales and Birkenhead from the direction of Shrewsbury, which became a key town in railway development in that period. During the second phase from 1861 to 1875, contractors often built railways then worked them independently or sold them on to the highest bidder. That process began after the money supply became more difficult for the bigger companies. Contractors built railways in areas where they were confident that large companies would be interested in buying them, either to secure their own position in a region, or to prevent a rival company from doing so. The Overend-Gurney banking crisis of 1866 then weakened the position of contractors who had taken on too much of the cost of development. The third phase from 1875 to 1885 was one in which companies – including the LNWR in north Wales – with capital to spare began to build lines for themselves once again. A minor fourth phase involved creating small scale projects in order to assuage local opinion as the right to vote

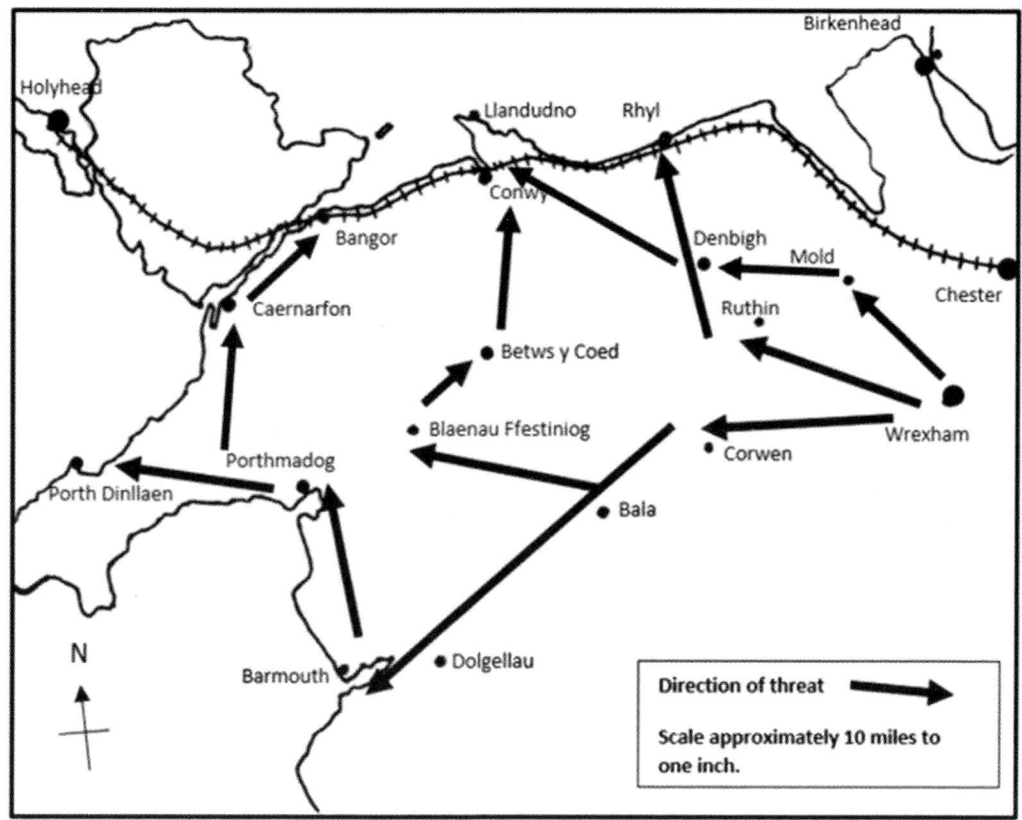

Map 1: Threats to the LNWR monopoly in North Wales c1850.

was extended to more men and political pressure on railway companies increased commensurately.

While government had supported the CHR and the LNWR up to 1850, it did not protect them from competition thereafter. Thus, the LNWR's powerful position weakened but without seriously affecting its dominance in north Wales. The first concern of the CHR while it was completing its own line between 1844 and 1850 was the development of rival services around Chester. As with its other concerns about competition, this was essentially because it wished to ensure that Holyhead had no serious rival. Parliament effectively destroyed the threat of a harbour and railway at Porth Dinllaen in 1846 when it supported the suppression of much of the broad-gauge expansion of the GWR. It simultaneously created a powerful rival to the GWR by approving the company amalgamations that produced the LNWR.

The formation of that company ended the squabbling that had occurred between the Liverpool-based Grand Junction Railway (GJR) and London and Birmingham

Railway (LBR) – with strong Manchester connections – which had reached its low point in 1844 when the GJR dropped out of the CHR because it lacked confidence in the latter's capacity to generate revenue to cover the burgeoning cost of the line and because the CHR had apparently attempted to purchase the Chester and Birkenhead Railway (CBR) without telling them.

The CBR was not a branch line of the CHR but did offer substantial access to the Irish traffic via a fast-growing port at Birkenhead that increasingly rivalled Liverpool where the GJR was dominant. The CHR was interested in buying this line from early 1844, but the CBR rejected its offer in December. The proposal created some opposition. The CBR chair noted in August 1844 that 'many parties had attempted to prejudice [the Board] against the purchase.' He was not specific about these parties, but the *Chester Chronicle* had no doubts. It commented in March 1845 that the amalgamation of the CBR and CHR was 'The first and all-important move of a great and important game against that *exclusive* Liverpool interest, [the GJR] which worked the railway and dock system for local instead of national purposes … for personal aggrandisement instead of imperial greatness.'

By March 1845, it was clear that the CHR was committed to extra spending on the Britannia Tubular Bridge, (BTB) and the government was offering less for the Irish mail contract than the CHR had expected. CBR shareholders were nervous, and the *North Wales Chronicle* told its readers on 18 March that its chair was suffering a 'perfect hell upon earth' under accusations that he was taking a 'double part' in the negotiations with the CHR. Before the next meeting he went to Italy for his health and missed the final decision to withdraw from the sale of the line to the CHR.

The CHR refused a revised proposal from the CBR, which then decided to oppose the Bill that joined the two companies. Investors were concerned about the health of the CHR and thought receiving payment in CHR shares was poor value. A furious row ensued, followed by a vote that committed the CBR to oppose amalgamation with the CHR.

The loss of the CBR was the first in a series of failures by the CHR, which was a proxy company for the LBR in these negotiations. That was clear in a government report that found that:

> There appear to us to be no sufficient public reasons to authorize such an amalgamation as that which is proposed [between the CBR and CHR because the CHR may] almost be considered as an extension of the LBR [and Birkenhead should not] be placed permanently and irrevocably under the exclusive control of a great Company.

After rejecting the CHR offer, the CBR was confident that it could survive independently, and concentrated on the situation south of Chester, where the North Wales Mineral Railway created a link between Wrexham and Chester in 1844. It soon became clear that a further extension towards Shrewsbury provided an opportunity to link Birkenhead with London via the GWR, a move that both the GJR and LBR – united in 1846 as part of the LNWR – feared.

Chester and Shrewsbury were highly strategic locations in this struggle, so were at the centre of a major dispute that began in 1849, and the LNWR kept Shrewsbury and Chester Railway (SCR) staff out of Chester's (nominally joint) station using 'rails, posts, bolts, chains ... stretching across the entrance of the road to the station'. In a debate on 27 May 1850, MPs accused the LNWR of being 'the leviathan of railway companies ... which exercised a huge and unjust monopoly, and lived upon litigation, selfishly and constantly oppressing the smaller companies.'

The SCR could not compete unaided with the might of the LNWR and between 1852 and 1854 joined with the Shrewsbury and Birmingham Railway and then combined with the GWR, the only company capable of resisting the LNWR. This coalition succeeded and by September 1854 the GWR had reached Birkenhead via its connections with its new allies in Shrewsbury, Chester, and Birmingham. The *Chester Chronicle* was supportive in its 2 September edition, noting that it hoped 'that nothing will occur on the part of the Birkenhead Company to prevent amicable traffic arrangements between the [GWR] and [the LNWR] and that the line from [Birkenhead] to Paddington, will be covered in six hours and a half.'

The GWR success in reaching Chester was certainly significant and provoked an aggressive and blustering response from the LNWR, the model for later reaction to developments it did not like, reported here in the *Chester Chronicle*:

> At the early part of the week, the Marquis of Chandos and Mr. Glyn, Directors of the [LNWR] paid a visit to Chester, and to Holyhead. [At] Birkenhead [they saw] that interesting locality [and] the details of a project for a new line from Chester to Birkenhead; and we understand that it is not unlikely that the [LNWR] will [support] such a line ... not that it is at all likely that the project is seriously entertained, or likely to obtain Parliamentary sanction; but the object doubtless is, to intimidate, if possible, the Birkenhead proprietors from entertaining an alliance with the [GWR]. It is a weak device that is, however, easily seen through.

In 1860, the LNWR and GWR wearied of the cost of their contest and agreed joint ownership of the line to Birkenhead.

The LNWR and CHR were more successful to the west of Chester in countering the threat of a line towards Mold that might have shortened the route to Holyhead or served another port in north Wales to Ireland. Plans for this railway were around during 1844, reported here by the *North Wales Chronicle* in July:

> There is every probability of railway being made to unite the town and neighbourhood of Mold with the Holyhead and Birkenhead Railways at Chester. The passenger traffic from the interior of North Wales, through Mold to Chester and Liverpool, is at present very considerable, and the fact that the vicinity of Mold abounds in coal, iron, limestone, lead, and other commodities, which only require a cheap outlet to the river Mersey and Liverpool, to become a valuable source of traffic, renders this railway a perfectly legitimate undertaking.

However, the interest of the CHR was more concerned with blocking rivals from the area such as the proposal to form a railway from the recently lost CBR at Hooton to Mold. The increasing costs of construction of the CHR put pressure on profits and by March 1849 it was unable to complete the purchase of the Mold Railway because of shareholder opposition.

LNWR Chair George Carr Glyn took over the process from the CHR to guarantee success. While other speakers tried to argue the case based on traffic expected on the line, Carr Glyn was concerned that if the CHR did not buy the Mold line then another railway company would, thereby damaging the LNWR's strategic and commercial interests. No doubt he had the GWR in mind. Carr Glyn persuaded a majority to support the acquisition – a result that suited the LNWR more than the CHR – thereby exposing the fiction of CHR independence.

The Mold line left the CHR at Saltney where there was a 'railway colony' – Mold Junction – with extensive sheds and slate sidings. There were stations at Broughton (Hall added to the title in 1861 then became Broughton and Bretton in 1908), Hope (Penyffordd added to the title in 1912) and Llong in 1849 with Padeswood (Buckley added to title 1894) opened in 1850 and Kinnerton and Saltney Ferry (Mold Junction) in 1891.

A spur from the Mold line supplied another good example of building a railway as a 'spoiler'. The 'Mold, Nerquis and Wrexham Railway' covered ground for a line from Wrexham towards the north Wales coast. Its lack of use from its original construction prompted the Mold Local Board to write to the LNWR in 1872. The Board 'believed the railway company had been in possession of the ground since 1847 ... *merely that other companies might be kept off*' [my emphasis].

Broughton and Bretton station was the first stop off the CHR towards Mold from 1849 until 1962. It was where Gladstone's funeral journey began in 1898. This picture is in 1961 as the end of passenger services neared. (© Ben Brooksbank cc-by-sa/2.0)

J. O. Binger, a senior LNWR manager, confirmed this when asked why the branch had not already opened to passengers, saying that he did not know 'why the d_ _d railway had been made in the place at all'. Another Board member explained the action, suggesting that the LNWR 'was acting the part of the dog in the manger. They had kept away [the GWR] and now refused to open the line after making it'.

The discussion so far has shown the rationale of the LNWR for acquiring branch lines in north Wales, a rationale that escaped people like Edmund Sharpe, whose focus was local advantage, and CHR shareholders who feared loss of dividend from the cost of branch lines. But promoting the construction of a line built to main-line standards on an unprofitable route was hardly an appealing prospect when the only beneficiary was the largest industrial corporation in the world, a status that followed the creation of the LNWR. Was there another advantage to which railway promoters could appeal when proposing branch lines in north Wales?

CHR shareholders objected to the purchase of the Mold Railway in 1849 and a senior manager could not explain why the company constructed the branch from it towards Wrexham. The two lines joined here at Tryddyn Junction near Mold, and both aimed to block off CHR rivals. **(WRRC)**

The Welsh Education Commissioners of 1847 supplied part of the answer. The government required a report to 'form some estimate of the general state of intelligence and information of the poorer classes in Wales.' The negative tone of the report was set by the introduction to it:

> My district exhibits the phenomenon of a peculiar language, isolating the mass from the upper portion of society; and, as a further phenomenon, it exhibits this mass engaged upon the most opposite occupations at points not very distant from each other; being on the one side rude and primitive agriculturalists, living poorly and thinly scattered; on the other, smelters and miners, wantoning in plenty and congregated in the densest accumulations.

The role of schools in north Wales was 'to teach the English Language … this [is] the standard by which the present condition of the schools in every particular must be estimated'. The arrival of the CHR had not helped. In Conwy, although 'the inhabitants have been greatly increased [by] the public works of the [CHR] no schools have been provided for the poor'. Aberffraw in Anglesey was 'the only parish upon the [CHR]… in which there is a school provided for the poor'. When a teacher wrote to the commissioners in Welsh that 'the railway [contractors took] the place where we hold [the school] and we have no place to hold it at present', the commissioners chose to criticise the teacher's use of Welsh, rather than the railway for commandeering the school house. Perhaps the ultimate criticism of the Welsh people was the hope the commissioners expressed that the influx of the notorious railway navvies would be a positive influence upon them because at least they spoke English.

Thus, the Education Commissioners unfairly viewed Welsh people as needing the blessings of the English way of life and especially the English language. Here was a hook for railway promoters in north Wales to hang the case for new railways in areas where there was little immediate economic benefit. As more railways were built in Wales, *The Times* noted triumphantly in 1863 that this was a modern invasion and conquest of Wales:

> The English were coming into Wales, not with bow and bills, but with money and locomotives, and the new invaders were more successful than the old ones. The parallel is indeed a curious one. … The halts of the British engineer have represented exactly the halts and stages of the Plantagenet Monarch … at Flint, at Rhyl, at Conway, at the Straits and at Carnarvon [he] built his castle at every station. The railway took up its track but has already exceeded its bounds. Edward could get no further than Carnarvon, but the iron rail is already beyond that mark, and will soon cross the very heart of Powysland from east to west.

There was one exception to the approach to branch line development outlined here, the notorious North Wales Railway (NWR), as distinct from the North Wales Mineral Railway from Chester to Wrexham. Henry Archer, who had made the case for a line to Porth Dinllaen from Shrewsbury in 1835, decided by April 1840 that the support for the coastal route from Chester was so strong that he should make a new proposal. He suggested that, after leaving Bangor, the line from Chester should not cross the Menai Straits but head for Caernarfon and then Porth Dinllaen. This was an intelligent move as he knew that the cost of crossing to

Mold was strategically important to the LNWR and eventually extended its links to Denbigh, Ruthin and Corwen. The company also created bus connections at the turn of the century which attracted much interest as is evident from this picture c1900. (John Alsop Collection)

Anglesey was high and an alternative once the railway line reached Bangor could be attractive. The CHR would then have become the Chester and Porth Dinllaen Railway. Thus, the NWR was born.

And far from opposing the scheme, the CHR was in 1846 the cause of a delay in NWR construction because it had altered the elevation of its own scheme to form a connection with the latter, the engineer of which was the well-respected Sir John Rennie. In March 1846, NWR shareholders heard that their line would open in July 1847. Henry Archer was notably absent from the meeting after the board dismissed him at the end of a complex dispute with David Williams, a solicitor acting for local landowners who had invested in the scheme.

By May 1847, all optimism had evaporated amid problems in the money market and concerns at rising costs. Rennie reduced the bill for his services but still expressed a view that the promotion of Holyhead as the main port would fail. However, rising optimism over the rail crossing to Anglesey dampened the enthusiasm for the NWR which became less attractive to financiers.

The dishonesty of two directors of the NWR, Secretary William Chadwick and Chair John Marriner – and the successful crossing of the Menai Straits – sank the project. They had interests in two other railway companies and illegally transferred funds from the NWR to those companies, a move regarded as venal even by the dubious standards of the railway world of the 1840s. They took steps to dissolve the NWR in February 1848 but then Henry Archer reappeared. Chadwick sued him for some of his claims, but Archer then took the matter to parliament with rather more success. In a debate in the Lords in July 1848, Lord Wharncliffe considered this to be 'One of the most scandalous cases that had occurred in the mismanagement of railways'. Archer probably intended to build the line to Caernarfon, unlike Chadwick and Marriner, whose efforts appear more akin to a Ponzi scheme, whereby money is moved around to give the appearance of a sound investment while the promoters use it to pay themselves handsomely.

From the perspective of the LNWR the outcome was satisfactory. While it was struggling to create a crossing to Anglesey, the NWR was a contingency for the CHR to secure the Irish traffic from Porth Dinllaen. Once the BTB was on course from around 1848, Euston was happy to see the NWR collapse without any action on its own part. But that was not the end of the LNWR's interest in a line to Caernarfon as we shall see.

Beginning with the skirmishes on the periphery, the LNWR demonstrated its determination to secure the whole of north Wales for itself and thereby protect the CHR. For that reason, it was unconcerned with the profitability of the various branch lines in the region. Later chapters will concentrate on the LNWR branches to the west of Mold and show how the strategic concerns of the LNWR were paramount and the interests of local communities and businesses less important. The LNWR sought to maximise its profits from transporting minerals, agricultural produce and people on the branch lines, but its focus was the coast and the risk that an incursion might challenge its hold on the lucrative Irish traffic.

Local dignitaries promoted other advantages to convince potential investors of the benefit of railways in the region. Among those advantages was 'modernisation' which in this context meant a challenge to the notion of Welshness and especially the value of the Welsh language. But there was another motivation in the early branch line developments, that Wales needed and deserved a railway system that focused on the needs of the Welsh economy and population, if necessary by challenging the power of Paddington and especially Euston. Key figures such as

Benjamin Piercy, Thomas Savin, David Davies, and Henry Robertson championed this approach in the first stage of railway development in the region.

By 1881, R.M. Preston, solicitor to the company, told an LNWR officers' dinner at Chester:

> There was not a single valley where a railway could go in this part of the country [Wales] in which the trains of the [LNWR] were not running'. He hoped that each employee: 'should never scruple to bear the mark of the [LNWR] on his collar when he knew it was a passport to society.'

Let us now see how this approach developed as the LNWR empire in north Wales expanded from Mold westwards and aimed 'to maintain their supremacy [in North Wales] for all time'.

Chapter 2

The Lines to Denbigh and the struggle for a third force in Welsh railways c1850-80

> Nothing tends more to clog our commerce and retard the development of our railway traffic than short independent lines.
> *Wrexham Advertiser,* 23 February 1867.

In the earlier chapter we noted how the GWR forged the link between Shrewsbury, Chester and Birkenhead and gained access to the Mersey and the Irish traffic. This was a period of great conflict between the LNWR and the GWR as the latter tried to win back the ground it lost with the decision of government to restrict the broad gauge after the Gauge Commission report in 1845. A glance at Map 1 shows the potential lines of attack for the GWR against the LNWR monopoly of traffic in north Wales west of Mold.

The conflict started along the Shrewsbury, Wrexham, Chester, and Birkenhead axis and spread westwards towards the next target town, which was Rhyl. The ground is steadily less suitable for railway construction to the west of Mold and necessarily channelled the competition into the valleys of the Dee, Clwyd, and Alun rivers. The map shows that the most promising direction for the feared GWR incursion was towards the towns of Ruthin and Denbigh from the SCR at Wrexham or Ruabon and thence northwards to Rhyl with its potential for both tourism and shipping links to Ireland and Liverpool.

There was a more complex route via Mold that approached Denbigh from the east along the Alun River. However, as we have seen, the LNWR had already secured a Chester to Mold route, so it preferred to concentrate on the districts to the south and east of Mold, particularly around Wrexham and Ruabon. Once the rivalry between the LNWR and the GWR reduced after 1860, they were jointly interested in resisting the rising demands for a distinct network of railways that connected north and south Wales and served the broader Welsh interests rather than

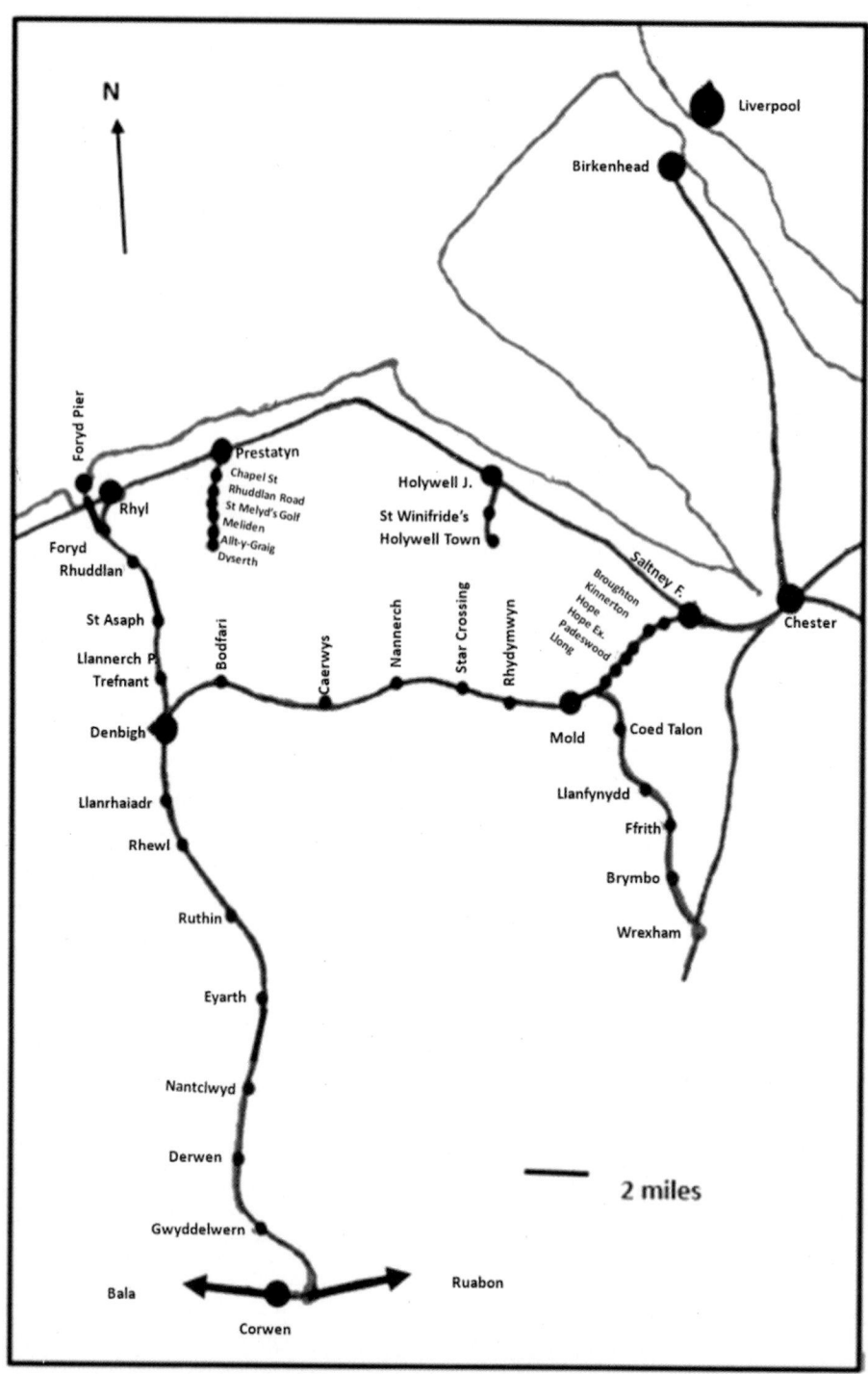

Map 2: LNWR branch lines in Flintshire and Denbighshire c1930.

the metropolitan railway elite. Control of Denbigh, Ruthin and Corwen was a vital part of that struggle. The story of railways to and from Denbigh is complicated as there were developments occurring simultaneously on several projects. Table 1 summarises the process.

The enthusiasm for railways in these districts was noted by the *Chester Chronicle* as early as September 1853 when a meeting in Ruthin considered three schemes: a direct line from Wrexham to Ruthin; an extension of that line via Denbigh to Rhyl; and a third rather circuitous line from Ruabon to Ruthin via Corwen and north to

	Vale of Clwyd	Denbigh, Ruthin and Corwen	Mold and Denbigh Junction
1855	Support from CHR		Opposed by LNWR
1856	Support from LNWR		
1858	Line opens		
1857	Battle for control of Board		
1859	LNWR nominees control the Board	Line proposed	
1860	Disputes on the Board		LNWR to build line
1861	Disputes on the Board	LNWR to operate it	Proposal abandoned
1862	Disputes on the Board	Open to Ruthin, LNWR operating it	Local interests promote the line
1863	LNWR controls line	Bridge over Dee at Corwen	Local interests promote the line
1864		Open to Corwen	Local interests promote the line
1865		Thomas Savin operates the line	Local interests promote the line
1866		Savin bankrupted and so DRCR runs it	Richard France asked to construct it
1867		Attempts to be part of Welsh railway amalgamation scheme. LNWR interests take control of the Board.	Tries to be part of Welsh railway amalgamation scheme. LNWR obstructing construction. Reneges on agreement to allow connections at Denbigh and Mold.
1868	Absorbed into LNWR	Line enters receivership	Construction
1869		Continues to operate its line	Line opens, operated by LNWR
1870			Nominal independence until 1923
1871		Out of receivership	
1878		LNWR operates the line	
1879		Absorbed into the LNWR	

Table 1: Timeline for the development of railway connections to Denbigh 1855-1879.

Rhyl. The report was less clear about likely supporters of these schemes but in October 1854 that mystery was solved at a further meeting in Ruthin chaired by local MP Frederick West of Chirk Castle.

He headed the list of local landowners backing a scheme for the 'Denbighshire Railway', taking the route that the earlier meeting rejected – Ruabon-Llangollen-Ruthin-Denbigh-St Asaph and Rhyl. The most important aspect of the scheme was the support expected from the GWR and there were connections with that company at the meeting, notably Thomas Mainwaring Penson, a prominent architect and surveyor who contributed to the impressive buildings on the SCR. West reported that the GWR was 'most friendly to the undertaking'.

When the committee reconvened two weeks later, it committed £448 towards a survey which expanded to £468 (£42,931) thanks to the increasingly enthusiastic Frederick West. Lord Bagot of Pool Park and Watkin Williams Wynn of Wynnstay Hall, who celebrated the GWR's success over the LNWR in reaching Chester, also contributed. They were the three wealthiest landowners in north Wales at that time. Interestingly, there were no contributions from Rhyl which was firmly in the grip of the LNWR.

It was lesser-known engineer and architect George Burnell who prepared the report on the Vale of Clwyd Railway (VCR) rather than Thomas Penson. In 1855 he reported favourably on a more limited project than the landowners of Ruthin had considered. He envisaged a line from Rhyl to Denbigh with an extension to Ruthin when finances allowed. It is notable that this scheme took the CHR as its starting point rather than the SCR which suggested the LNWR would support it. Burnell reinforced that notion with his telling comment, reported in the *North Wales Chronicle* of 27 October, that:

> The Vale of Clwyd exports the bulk of its agricultural produce to Liverpool or to the manufacturing districts of Cheshire, either by the Coasters [merchant ships] or by the [CHR]. At present there does not appear to exist any business connection between the vale and the south-east parts of the main land, a circumstance that is easily accounted for by the natural barrier of the mountainous districts at its head which affords another illustration of the adage that commerce follows the course of the streams.

By the time of this report, Burnell had lodged his assessment with a solicitor in Rhyl who advertised in the *Chester Courant* for 'Country gentlemen … disposed to divide their attention fairly between the existing means of traffic (Turnpike Roads) and the Railways [and take] a sufficient amount of shares to make them eligible as directors.' A month later a committee met and then posted a notice in the same newspaper that it would build a line from Rhyl to Denbigh with the full cooperation of the CHR.

Opposition to the scheme was not initially from the direction of Wrexham and Ruabon but from those suggesting that the best way of connecting Denbigh and Chester was through extending the Mold Railway west to Denbigh. This was not a project that appealed to the LNWR as the company was suspicious of any line running parallel to the CHR offering a rival route from Chester towards Rhyl and beyond. However, in 1855 the Euston company did not oppose the scheme. But the promoters had the deity behind them as the Reverend W.H. Owen told the meeting at St Asaph in February 1856 that he considered 'Railways as the pioneers of Religion as well as of Civilization generally'.

The CHR approach to branch lines was more pragmatic as the CHR chair Sir Samuel Morton Peto explained to shareholders in 1856:

> I believe that the subject of branch line railways has been very much misunderstood in this country, more so than in any other. ... In the first place, the branches have been constructed [to guard existing traffic rather than produce traffic]. Where they have been constructed in the right direction ... have been made without sufficient reference to the local parties, and without making them parties to the expenditure. The consequence has been that branches have cost very much more than they would have done if they had been constructed in the right direction; and where they have been constructed in the wrong direction, they have been so costly they have tended to produce a universal feeling or wish to avoid all branches of any kind whatsoever. ... Then with regard to the line, which I am very desirous to see secured, from Denbigh to St. Asaph [and Rhyl], we are quite prepared, if the landowners construct that branch, to make very liberal arrangements. I have conferred with the [LNWR] board and officers upon the subject, and they quite concur in our views, and we shall get considerable benefit from the traffic.

In the 1850s and 1860s, large companies tended to allow contractors to complete lines and then bought or controlled them if it was in their interest to do so. That meant that large companies did not have to find the money to develop the lines. But there were drawbacks. Principal among these was the tendency for contractors to spot lines that large companies wanted, build them, and then watch the price of sale escalate as the railway titans battled for control. The VCR was a perfect example of the process. It was the gateway to Rhyl and the coast and whichever company gained control could then determine the direction south of Denbigh. We have seen that under GWR control the VCR would continue south via Ruthin towards Ruabon, while under LNWR management the line might not extend south or if it did would tend towards Corwen, meaning that the route from Ruabon to Rhyl was lengthy and inconvenient.

The bitter dispute between the GWR and LNWR – part of the wider 'railway war' – held up the development of the VCR. So, the 'Provisional Committee' of local people struggled to make progress in 1855-56. The first share offers failed and there was opposition from road and river operators and the CHR. Once it was clear that the VCR's Act of Parliament would include shared arrangements with the CHR and LNWR, the process became a little easier, though local money to support the project was still insufficient. And when the legislation came before committee in February 1856, there was nobody there to present it.

It was only when local MP Townshend Mainwaring took over the chair of the faltering committee later in 1856 that the scheme made progress. His position was interesting. He was the local MP but also on the board of the Rhyl Hotel Company alongside Morton Peto and Richard Preston, who was solicitor to the CHR. That company intended to construct a hotel to take advantage of the growing tourist potential of Rhyl. Mainwaring's election as chair suggested success for the LNWR in any battle for control of the VCR, as the CHR's independence of the Euston company was nominal. But there was a tension at the heart of the project in the form of the engineering partnership of Benjamin Piercy, David Davies, and Thomas Savin, whose were closer to the GWR.

Savin hailed from the Welsh border country and had a keen sense of identity with Wales and the needs of its economy. He began his engineering career around 1857 to build the VCR and did so in partnership with David Davies who became a major figure in Welsh Liberal politics, while Savin became a Conservative from 1870. Piercy was also a powerful figure in Welsh life but with more of a focus on economic development. He was associated closely with Henry Robertson, another prominent Liberal politician. Although originating from Scotland, Robertson was committed to economic development in north Wales, particularly around the Wrexham area where he headed the Brymbo Iron Foundry. Together these men formed a powerful counterweight to the LNWR. Though relations between them were not always cordial, they had a consistent focus on the economic and social needs of north Wales, and their deaths between 1888-90 were a great loss to the region.

If there were tensions around the creation of the VCR, they were not clear at the 'cutting of the sod' ceremony in August 1857 with Piercy merely remarking that the line was preferable to the alternative line from Denbigh to Mold. Construction of the line was generally uncomplicated, but no opportunity was lost to boost its commercial value, such as this snippet in the local papers in May 1858 concerning 'indications of mineral wealth':

> In making excavations upon a large scale at the Graig lime quarry [near Denbigh] for the purpose of raising stone for the construction of the viaducts on the [VCR] a magnificent vein of quartz, of several yards thick and unknown depth, has been partially laid bare ... Indications of the presence of copper, *if not of gold ore,* [my emphasis] are in many specimens unmistakable.

In October 1858, the line opened with intermediate stations at Rhuddlan, Trefnant and St Asaph. The VCR also agreed to supply a private halt for Whitehall Dod of Llannerch Park, a director of the VCR. There were elaborate ceremonies at Denbigh, St Asaph, and Rhyl. Dignitaries joined the train in Denbigh and travelled northwards behind two 0-4-2 saddle tanks built by Sharp Stewart and called *Clwyd* and *Elwy*, 'well-called the harbingers of commerce and civilization' according to the account in the *North Wales Chronicle*. It noted the enthusiasm of St Asaph and the 'indifference' of Rhuddlan, where shipping interests had opposed the line, and the station was at the bottom of a hill and some distance from the town. There was greater enthusiasm and long speeches at Rhyl. The Lord Bishop of St Asaph blessed the railway and commented favourably on the conduct of the navvies who built it.

Rhuddlan station was not close to the town centre and affected local shipping, so there was sparse celebration in the town when it opened in 1858. In this 1966 picture there is little sign of railway business apart from camping coaches in the siding. (RCTS Photo Archive: collection of Jack Faithfull)

However, Mr E G Salisbury, MP for Chester, introduced a controversial note when he revealed his own ambition for the project, unsurprisingly not reported in Welsh papers but in the *Chester Chronicle*:

> Every Welshman who feels thoroughly an interest in the welfare of his country will do what he can to promote not only this, but every other line tending to bring about the renovation of our race. How is the renovation of the Welsh race to be brought about? By the promotion of railways. I, for one, am not ashamed to say—and I say it here boldly—that I shall be delighted to see the Welsh People Anglicized. I am quite sure that the way to Anglicize the Welsh people is by the promotion of railways and commerce among them and making the English and Welsh thoroughly and completely one people.

The directors' concerns were more tangible. They knew that the survival of the VCR as a private company was not a long-term option and so kept infrastructure and traffic costs low, reported here in *Herapath's Railway Journal* of 1 December 1858:

> The Directors contracted with Messrs Savin and Davies for sleepers, ballasting, and laying the permanent way. The amount of the contract is £10,000. [£1.02M] The same firm is also constructing stations and sidings at a schedule of prices. The Directors have been fortunate in being enabled to purchase the rails at a low price. It being desirable to work the line with your own rolling stock, locomotives designed specifically for the purpose have been built … and carriages, wagons, and vans, have been built and supplied by Mr John Ashbury [of Manchester]. Stations are on an economical scale [consistent] with deeming it more prudent to increase the accommodation as the traffic demands it.

More likely it was to keep their own costs low and leave the task of developing the line to the company that bought it from them. Their initial task was to ensure that the price of the line was as high as possible by maintaining the interest of both the LNWR and GWR. They did this by suggesting they could develop the line in several directions. 'It is in contemplation to extend [the VCR] to Ruthin, still more southward, and thence to the picturesque district of Llangollen, and [to the GWR] at Llangollen Road station [Ruabon].'

A larger railway transaction strengthened the position of the LNWR on 30 December 1858 when it bought the CHR thus formalising its control. The LNWR through the CHR then made clear its intention to extend the VCR by controlling the Denbigh, Ruthin, and Corwen Railway [DRCR], thus preventing any direct connection to the GWR at Ruabon. A notice issued in November 1859 confirmed that the DRCR would work directly with the CHR and the VCR. And the LNWR controlled access of the VCR into Rhyl as a bargaining chip.

For the first two years of its existence, the VCR stopped at Foryd, a mile short of Rhyl, thus frustrating passengers who wished to join the CHR at Rhyl or the steamers from Foryd to Liverpool. The steamer *Lion,* owned by James Napier and Thomas Savin, attracted much business and they were important promoters of the VCR. They worked with Hugh Robert Hughes of Kinmel, owner of the land at Foryd next to the CHR. His solution to accessing the pier was to run a line from the VCR under the CHR so that VCR passengers could embark for Liverpool or cross by ferry into Rhyl. Hughes would not assure the LNWR that he would not use the line for commercial purposes and so it forcibly ejected his workers from its property in the summer of 1859.

Extensive court action followed. The LNWR won the first case and Hughes the second. The *North Wales Chronicle* sided with Hughes and the VCR and suggested that the LNWR obstructed the development through fear of losing its traffic to Liverpool.

The battle between the various interests paved the way for the LNWR's acquisition of the VCR, though the process is opaque. A notice appeared in the press

Initially the VCR stopped at Foryd a few hundred yards from the CHR. In this 1953 picture the two tracks on the left are from Foryd Junction, on the main line from Rhyl. The track in the centre is the original VCR line to Foryd Pier. On the right is the line to Kinmel Camp. **(LNWR Society)**

The Foryd Pier branch from the north side of the CHR with a train (or stored coaches) on the VCR in the background, and an engineer's train of 4-wheel flat wagons on the pier branch in 1953. (LNWR Society)

outlining the VCR's intentions in December 1859. It was for the 'construction of a railway from the Foryd station of the [VCR] to Rhyl; construction of a railway and toll-bridge across the river at Foryd; powers to run over the [CHR] from the Foryd junction to the Rhyl station on that railway, and for the use of the Rhyl station.'

During May and June 1860 Mainwaring and two other directors reported they had attended meetings in London and mysteriously agreed to LNWR running powers over the VCR in return for the use of LNWR facilities. They had done so apparently as the only means of getting their own legislation agreed. The effect was to weaken GWR interest in the VCR and the Foryd Pier extension since it would be unable to access it. Some shareholders alleged that the VCR secretary Robert Roberts acted both for the VCR and the LNWR and after completing the deal accepted a lucrative post with the East India Company. Hughes of Kinmel had by then conceded that the LNWR was too big an opponent to defeat and compromised. Another shareholder was in no doubt about the LNWR's motive as reported in the *Wrexham Advertiser* on 26 May 1860:

> Now their position was a very critical one. The [LNWR] were very anxious to lease the line. Why so anxious on the point now? Would they not be as anxious next year to get a lease of the line when the traffic was more developed? Then what was the object? Why to block up the Vale ("No, no") Yes it was, he could see it very plainly.

This tension within the VCR board reached its peak in September 1860 when the meeting was particularly fractious. There had been significant changes on the board with the arrival of Robert Gardner, a wealthy investor from Manchester, and Thomas Hughes of Ystrad, an important local politician and landowner. The Board appointed Martin Smith, an experienced railwayman with the Great Northern, as manager of the VCR but, like Gardner, he had no obvious connection to the area. There appeared to have been irregularity or neglect of accounts in this period that caused Thomas Savin successfully to seek an adjournment of the meeting.

At the later meeting, the essential differences among the shareholders and directors became clearer. Both Savin and Piercy attended, and a fierce argument ensued between those who advocated for a line that directed traffic towards the CHR and the Foryd pier extension and those who thought the line should develop south within a wider network of railways that served the more general interests of Wales. Savin attacked what he saw as the directors' extravagant spending on infrastructure and the Foryd extension, while Piercy exposed what he considered as the strategic errors in the plan, reported here in the *North Wales Chronicle*:

> He had attended there in the interest of the extension of their railway through the heart of Wales. He was pledged to those extensions over and over again and it was therefore his duty not to give way to his feelings ... He looked upon the [VCR] as a mere link in an important system of railway which he hoped soon to see developed in North Wales. ... It was [the directors'] general policy he blamed them for – that foolish Foryd Extension Bill, and the working expenses, which were at least 25 per cent higher than was necessary.

It was all to no avail. The reformed Board persuaded the shareholders to support the direction it had set. Savin and Piercy could not force a further adjournment and the later special meeting agreed to approach parliament for powers to raise more capital.

By March 1861, the VCR meetings were calmer because Savin and Piercy were absent and the drift towards ownership by the LNWR was underway. Attendance was small and Gardner was happy to appoint a deputy because he 'could not enter into the details of the company minutely'. In truth it was because he had completed his work for the LNWR. That meeting noted that Savin had promoted a rival line to Foryd Pier and there was a bill before parliament for a another line to Denbigh – the Mold and Denbigh Junction Railway [MDJR]. The VCR Board opposed both developments and were confident that the competing line to Foryd would fail – and they were right.

These negotiations over the VCR took place at a time when the LNWR and GWR were in a bitter conflict over the CBR, as we saw in the last chapter. It seems possible that half the VCR board was working to keep the LNWR interested, notably Mainwaring and Secretary Roberts, while the other half, led by Savin, was urging for the GWR. The collapse of GWR interest occurred at precisely the time that the conflict between the LNWR and GWR ended, and they agreed to shared ownership of the CBR in November 1860, as the *Liverpool Daily Post* reported:

> The pending transfer of the [CBR] to the [LNWR] and [GWR] is likely in the next session to become [complete]. After a display of an amount of virulence scarcely paralleled in railway warfare, the two great companies have agreed to a truce, and the [CBR] ... is now likely to be taken over with a guaranteed dividend.

The direction of travel for the VCR from the start was consistently towards closer alliance with the LNWR – encouraged by the Euston guarantee of a 5 per cent return on shares – and support for connecting lines towards Mold, Corwen and Foryd Pier. The notion that a desire to raise the share price drove the actions of the majority of directors of the VCR was supported in May 1861 with a report that Gardner, the new VCR chairman, who held over a third of its shares, was offered 10 per cent above the premium by the LNWR and accepted, apparently without consulting his colleagues on the board. His move put Euston in such a strong position that it soon secured control of the VCR.

In addition to this benefit, Gardner had also commissioned the steamer *Denbigh* from Lairds of Birkenhead in 1860, intending to run a fast service between Foryd Pier and Liverpool, challenging the *Lion* – owned by former directors and rivals Napier and Savin. The *Denbigh* soon saw more exciting action after Gardner sold it on to the Confederate States as a blockade runner during the American Civil War and the Union forces sank it near Galveston in 1865.

So, despite the various manoeuvres of Savin, Piercy, and others it never seemed likely that the VCR would end up anywhere but within the control of the LNWR, as Townshend Mainwaring – who had chaired the company at a crucial time – let slip to the *North Wales Chronicle*:

> He was glad that arrangement with the [LNWR] was carried out. He had only had shares in two railways in the whole kingdom, one of which was their own little line and the other the [LNWR] and he was happy to see them amalgamated. He was glad to see the Foryd extension was to be carried out, and there was great traffic to be derived from it. He was satisfied with all that was done.

And doubtless satisfied with the guarantee of a 5 per cent return on his shares. Secretary Roberts did, as alleged, obtain lucrative employment as an auditor with the East India Company, but died of disease in Alexandria on his way home to retirement in 1878.

By 1863, LNWR figures such as James Bancroft (a director of the LNWR), Richard Preston (Solicitor LNWR), and Charles Stewart (LNWR Goods Traffic Manager) dominated the VCR Board, and the materials for the Foryd Pier Extension were in place. Although most accounts suggest that passenger services did not extend to the pier station, there was a trip to Liverpool in August 1864 on the steamer *Ruby* which included a rail journey to the 'Foryd Pier station' so the line was clearly open by then. Once the VCR was connected to Rhyl, Foryd station was less important and closed in 1885.

Looking towards the road crossing from Foryd Pier in 1959. The line passes under the CHR a few hundred yards beyond the crossing. **(The Transport Treasury)**

In 1959, a hundred years after the furore over access to Foryd engulfed the VCR, the lines and the harbour sheds are derelict. (The Transport Treasury)

The prize for the VCR was connection to the CHR and access to Rhyl. The junction is clear in this picture looking towards Rhyl with the VCR joining from the right c1953. (LNWR Society)

Even before the VCR finally moved to the LNWR, an argument raged about the direction of any extension to it, though all agreed that Ruthin was the first target. At the heart of the issue was how Llangollen and Ruabon should access Ruthin and Denbigh. There were two proposals, a 'high line' that passed to the north of Llangollen to Pentrefelin, and a rival from Henry Robertson with a station close to the river and the town centre. The GWR supported the latter scheme, which the LNWR therefore opposed.

The rival engineers and landowners battled the issue in parliamentary committees and public meetings where Robertson gained the upper hand in technical arguments. He pressed local landowner George Hammond Whalley of Plas Madoc Hall about his opposition to the low line and Whalley admitted to material help from the LNWR and a bias against the New British Iron Company which challenged his own commercial interests and supported Robertson's line. The cross examination also exposed a plan to convert the Llangollen canal into a railway as part of the LNWR scheme. Robertson proved to be a most effective opponent of the LNWR's monopolistic ambitions. A typically sharp comment from him was that a railway in the area that did not serve the New British Iron Company (at Acrefair) would be like 'a performance of the play of Hamlet with the part of Hamlet left out.'

A noisy and acrimonious public meeting in April 1859 was convinced that the LNWR was behind Whalley's opposition to Robertson and that the so-called 'high line' involving canal destruction was a fiction, or, if built, a 'spoiler' line with little practical value. Local churchwarden Robert Baker encapsulated this view in his proposal:

> That this meeting having heard the explanations relating to the position of the Vale of Llangollen Railway bill, pledges itself to support its progress through the House of Lords and is opposed to the suggested scheme of the Canal Conversion as destructive of a useful navigation, and as an attempt to place the communication though the Vale in the hands of the [LNWR] who have no railway connection with the district. That they regard the scheme of Canal Conversion as an attempt to deprive the district of all railway accommodation and merely originated to frustrate the efforts of the Vale of Llangollen Railway, consisting of parties interested in the district and locally connected by residence, property, and trade.

The resolution passed unanimously and is a correct account of the LNWR's approach to controlling railway development in the region. The 'low-level' Vale of Llangollen Railway received parliamentary approval in August 1859. We have cause to be thankful that the high-level line failed, and the Llangollen canal survived as a World Heritage Site.

Once it could not prevent access to the interior of Denbighshire from the SCR at Ruabon, the LNWR focus shifted to where the Llangollen line might go next. A westerly extension was the obvious development for the GWR and its allies, so the LNWR aimed to reach Corwen first, as the town supplied three routes that could trouble it: Denbigh towards Rhyl; Betws-y-Coed towards Llandudno; and Bala towards Porth Dinllaen via Ffestiniog or Barmouth.

It was consistent with LNWR policy on branch lines that it did not build the line from Denbigh to Corwen itself. There was no great response from local investors, but Messrs Piercy, Davies and Savin supplied most of the finance, hoping for a good return from the rivalry between the GWR and LNWR. The strategic status of the Denbighshire line in the ongoing 'railway war' and its potential within a wider Welsh network, were emphasised by the *North Wales Chronicle* when Florence West of Ruthin Castle cut the first sod of the line from Llangollen to Corwen in September 1860:

> It is part of a system which is intended to give the GWR access to Rhyl, already a place of some note as a fashionable resort and destined at no distant day to become a packet station and mercantile port of considerable importance. From Corwen it is intended to branch off to Ffestiniog and Barmouth and there to connect North and South Wales by means of a coastal line extending from Newtown and Machynlleth at the latter to Portmadoc, Pwllheli, Porthdinllaen and Carnarvon.

The first meeting of the DRCR board was in January 1861, when Benjamin Piercy reported on slow progress caused by lack of access to land. Captain Jasper Wilson Johns, a civil engineer and politician, elaborated further. 'About four miles of the road is almost ready for the sleepers, and sleepers are on the ground for about seven miles of railway ... the question of completion between here and Denbigh is simply a matter of land.'

The 'matter of land' was a polite reference to the obstruction to the route from the Myddleton-West family at Ruthin Castle. They objected because the route was too close to their palatial residence and so insisted on changes. Originally, the line ran along the low-lying land to the west of Ruthin. The station was then located on the western side of the town but had to shift to the east. There was extra cost from an extensive cutting and duplication of buildings already constructed along the original route.

By the next meeting, the notion of the line forming part of the GWR system in north Wales ended as shareholders heard of an agreement with the LNWR. The chair told the meeting that this exercised 'a material influence over the policy that ought to be pursued in the management of our railway'. He outlined two examples of that influence, the withdrawal of the proposed line from Denbigh to Mold and continued opposition to a GWR proposal for a line from Corwen to Bala.

The LNWR used the same method it had applied on the VCR; it guaranteed a return of 4.5 per cent on capital, though few thought that level was possible on the DRCR. The line opened as far as Ruthin on 1 March 1862 with huge celebrations in the town. The rest of the line did not open in the summer as hoped. Piercy reported in September that there were still difficulties accessing land, heavy works at Eyarth and delays to the bridge over the Dee at Corwen.

The cutting at Eyarth proved especially difficult and costly to the workers. Moses Hughes of Denbigh died after a mishap with dynamite on 22 November 1861. Charles Knight from Somerset was in the cutting on 3 June 1862 when a rockfall buried him and he died in Corwen a few hours later.

The Dee crossing opened a year later, and the experience of the navvies was better than at Eyarth, as reported here by the *North Wales Chronicle*:

> On the 30th [April] the first railway truck went over the new bridge across the Dee, under the charge of Mr. Geo. Beckingham, one of the sub-contractors on the [DRCR]. The navvies were on the bridge at the time, waving their hats and giving hearty cheers, also hundreds of the townspeople were taking the opportunity of witnessing the first waggon going over. Ale in abundance was supplied to the navvies on the success of their undertaking. In a very short time, it is expected the rails will be laid down up to the town. The Llangollen and Corwen line, it is rumoured, will not be open for traffic for twelve months, on account of Berwyn tunnel.

The Dee was a major obstacle to reaching Corwen until contractors completed a bridge in 1863, seen here with the engineers' carriage hauled by a Trevithick 6ft single locomotive. (LNWR Society)

A year later the contractors continued to struggle at Eyarth with a heavy toll on the navvies. Herbert Jones hurt himself seriously when he fell between loaded trucks. But the *North Wales Chronicle* thought the price was worth paying:

> There have now three been killed since the commencement of this cutting, and a great many hurt, but we are happy to think that we are not likely to hear of any such accident again in this cutting, and that we shall soon see the old iron horse puffing and smoking along the way to this town.'

But Morris Williams, who gave up driving the local mail coach to work on the line, did not see the first train as he died under spoil trucks at Eyarth in April 1864.

The LNWR had won the race to Corwen, although the formal opening did not occur until October 1864 and was a muted affair with few railway dignitaries or local landowners present. South from Denbigh, the line had stations at Llanrhaiadr, Rhewl, Ruthin, Eyarth, Nantclwyd, Derwen, and Gwyddelwern. The lack of excitement at its formal opening may have been because locals used the line in August 1864, when an enterprising local charged:

> 3s 6d [£15] the double journey, to the Llandudno Eisteddfod [and] a train of thirty carriages and two engines left here at 7.40 a.m., with 130 excursionists … a vast concourse of people met to hail its appearance, and as it glided slowly over the Dee Bridge (which is here called 'the monster bridge') loud shouts of joy rent the air.

Although formal hostilities between the LNWR and the GWR had ceased, relations between them were far from cordial as shown by the first station arrangements in Corwen. The DRCR terminus was in the town centre but the Llangollen and Corwen station was further west and less convenient.

It is necessary to examine the MDJR development to fully understand the emergence of railway construction in this sub-region of north Wales. Railway promoters aired the idea of a connection between Mold and Denbigh several times to improve the Chester to Denbigh journey time but the scheme had not progressed. Neither had it gone away. In 1860, the *North Wales Chronicle* hoped 'shortly to see the line [at Mold] extended to Denbigh, by which means a most extensive trade will be opened out. We are informed that several influential gentlemen and landowners are desirous of this extension and will give it their cordial support'. On 17 November 1860, the DRCR published its intention to build a railway but withdrew it when it understood that the LNWR would construct the line.

The DRCR meeting in September 1861 was tense, and in subsequent months the arrangements at the company deteriorated. Attendance at the meeting in September 1862 was much reduced but relations with the LNWR good enough for Euston to operate the line between Denbigh and Ruthin. Two years later there was a meeting, but no business transacted. By September 1865 there was a new arrangement with the GWR that was said to be working well apart from the need to change trains at Denbigh when travelling from Corwen towards Rhyl. The DRCR then took over management of the line and Thomas Savin operated it.

There was clearly something amiss in the business of the DRCR. As usual, the LNWR's determination to keep control over developments in the region was part of the process. Thomas Savin's financial difficulties increased, worsened by his tendency to take payment for his construction work in shares rather than cash. Through this process he amassed huge debts and by February 1866 he had to call in receivers.

1866 saw the great financial crash centred on the Overend Gurney Bank, with railway debts at the heart of the problem. Railway contractors' debts were particularly marked when they constructed short lines and quickly exceeded the borrowing powers, exactly the kind of work Savin had undertaken. The most immediate impact on the DRCR was that it had to take over the operation of the line from Savin. It showed some enterprise by turning its attention west as well as north and offering 'sea-bathing' tickets for the Cambrian coast. But it offered no dividend to shareholders in August 1866.

Significantly, the DRCR was part of a wider development in Welsh railways in 1866 that alarmed the LNWR. This was the 'report issued by the committee of debenture and shareholders meeting in London to promote the amalgamation of Welsh railways [in which] it does not appear that the union [of Welsh railways] scheme will be seriously supported in Parliament during the ensuing session.' A merger of the DRCR and MDJR was part of these developments as were the 'hostile movements … on the part of other companies.' The DRCR and MDJR certainly felt the force of these hostile movements when they proposed a merger which was a direct challenge to Euston as the *Wrexham Advertiser* noted:

> The [DRCR] a line at present only 19 miles in length but destined at no distant day to form a link in what may not inaptly be called "The Welsh Midland Railway", for we understand that the company are promoting a bill in the present Parliament, which has already passed its preliminary stages, for amalgamating with the [MDJR], and for the construction of short length between Mold and Padeswood, with running powers from thence to Chester.

The company already possess running powers between Corwen and Dolgelly, so that if the scheme passes its integrity – and there are good reasons for anticipating that it will —this line would form continuous and unbroken route between Chester and Aberystwyth—a desideratum much needed, for nothing tends more to clog our commerce and retard the development of our railway traffic than short independent lines, with their numerous termini, and consequent delay and annoyance to the public.

The proposed amalgamation cleared the Commons in May 1867, which spurred the LNWR to frustrate it. A committee hearing in May 1867 exposed the methods employed by Euston when members heard that the smaller company had abandoned its proposal. Richard France explained the process. He was a contractor like Thomas Savin and built part of the MDJR at his own expense, taking shares as payment. Like Savin he sank into financial difficulties because of this approach. He told the committee that the MDJR and DRCR wanted to amalgamate 'but certain shareholders of the [DRCR] are interested in the [LNWR] and they put the pressure on, and thus the amalgamation part of the scheme had to be abandoned.'

He was referring to James Ashbury, who bought a large shareholding and joined the DRCR Board. This was a similar tactic to that used by the LNWR on the VCR, where James Bancroft suddenly became involved and steered the company in Euston's direction. The committee heard that Ashbury was not an LNWR shareholder but that he was acting in its interest: a suggestion that was hardly in doubt as the *North Wales Chronicle* noted just a week after the committee meeting that he 'some months ago [showed] his determination to the resist the proposed amalgamation of Welsh railways as impolitic and premature, but he fully and heartily cooperates in the modified arrangements for working these several lines.' 'Several' meant separate in this context. Additionally, Ashbury was proprietor of a vast railway wagon works in Manchester, and it seems inconceivable that the LNWR was not one of his largest customers, and a company that he was happy to assist.

The committee heard the catalogue of obstructionist tactics employed by the LNWR against the MDJR. By denying access to either Mold or Denbigh it had 'blocked up the [MDJR] at every end' and forced the small company to seek access to other lines such as the Wrexham Mold and Connah's Quay Railway [WMCQR] at one end and the DRCR at the other. The shareholders had got Richard France to build the line because the LNWR had reneged on a promise to do so. France told the committee that the whole district favoured the development of the MDJR, but the LNWR used its power and wealth to 'weary out' the smaller company and frustrate the scheme. The committee granted power to the MDJR to access Denbigh but denied running powers over LNWR and WMCQR lines at its eastern end.

The process by which the LNWR secured effective control of the MDJR – they never actually absorbed it – included an episode that exposed the attitude of Euston towards railway developments in north Wales and the connection of those railways to the rest of Wales. We have seen already that the LNWR had obstructed the work of Richard France on the MDJR. Despite those efforts the MDJR had won its parliamentary battle and France had constructed the line in time to prevent the loss of a £10,000 (£926,000) deposit by the promoters of the MDJR. The LNWR forced the MDJR to construct a separate access to Mold at the eastern end of its line but had allowed no access to the VCR in either direction. The MDJR took its case to parliament and eventually the LNWR said it had withdrawn its opposition and the matter appeared closed.

Then Lord Redesdale – a man with an influential position in railway legislation, and unorthodox views on a range of topics – took the unusual step of inserting a clause that blocked the MDJR access to the LNWR system without any reference to the parliamentary committees or the promoters of the bill. He did so at the request of an LNWR solicitor who had not previously appeared before the committee but waited for all parties to leave before approaching Lord Redesdale.

Richard France reacted furiously by producing a pamphlet in 1867 titled *Lord Redesdale and the New Railways,* which took his lordship to task over his attitude towards contractor-funded railways. France pointed out the railway mania of 1844-46 wrecked the old subscription system that had funded the growth of railways in the 1840s. Subsequent railway promoters had to provide a deposit on the completion of their Act of Parliament and agree to start work within a specified period, often one year. During the 1860s this approach enabled work to start but then contractors had to compensate for lack of local funding by taking on the cost of the work in return for promised benefits once the line opened. We have seen that approach in the lines discussed in this chapter with Thomas Savin, David Davies, and Benjamin Piercy prominent. France pointed out that Redesdale's wish to return to the old system effectively prevented the building of new lines in rural areas such as north Wales which did not yield large returns on investments.

Redesdale's approach was, of course, welcomed by the big operators like the LNWR which wanted to avoid competition and had little interest in developing rural areas. France showed that the LNWR had initially backed the MDJR and provided a deposit for its construction and it had done so to thwart the VCR. However, once it had secured the VCR for itself, it then took no action to construct the MDJR and began to oppose its construction. Redesdale's colleague peers supported him, but one noted in a debate in the Lords on 11 March that, 'about £200,000, [£18.4M] he understood, had been already expended upon the railway, which, however, would under this clause be entirely delivered up to the mercy of the great Company which opposed it, unless another Act of Parliament were passed on the subject'.

Redesdale's action seems inexplicable, short of bribery by the LNWR. If that notion appears fanciful, it is worth recalling Sir John Gladstone's (William Gladstone's father and a beneficiary of slavery compensation) account (published in the *Daily Post* after his death in 1851) of how the Liverpool and Manchester Railway (LMR) Act passed: 'When the [LMR] scheme was before parliament, I was one of the directors, and I assure you, upon my honour, that we never should have succeeded if we had not taken the precaution of bribing every member of the House of Commons committee.'

There is no evidence of bribery in this case, but Redesdale's actions were extraordinary and ensured the LNWR could prevent any independent rail link encroaching on its core regional area of operation – Flintshire, Denbighshire, Caernarvonshire, and Anglesey. It did so by only agreeing to the connections to its network if it ran the line. The MDJR opened in September 1869 after a deal in Chancery to raise the money and two contractors from Wigan engaged to finish the work. The line was 15.5 miles long with four stations west from Mold; Rhydymwyn, Nannerch, Caerwys and Bodfari and it cut the journey distance from Chester to Denbigh from 31.5 (via Rhyl) to 19 miles, though the journey times were similar.

Soon after the committee hearing in parliament it was reported that Ashbury was manoeuvring to become chairman of the DRCR. He was fully supported by the *Railway Times* which noted in October 1867, 'The extreme folly of waging war with the [LNWR] … must be exhibited in its true colours as well as in its inevitable results.' Ashbury continued his attack into 1868 and secured the appointment of a sub-committee nominated by him to investigate the company. The company was in receivership in the first half of 1868 before large Manchester and Liverpool-based shareholders with Ashbury as chair took control of the board. The DRCR connected to Mold at the northern end in 1869 with the LNWR working that line – the MDJR – and it came out of receivership in 1871.

By that time, the idea of creating a through route from north to south Wales as part of an independent Welsh rail network had disappeared in line with the aims of both the LNWR and the GWR. The DRCR continued its operations under its own management and provided a return of around 4 per cent until 1878 when the LNWR chair Richard Moon told his shareholders of a new arrangement to work the DRCR. The change came in July via an imperious visit by LNWR officials, to the manifest delight of the populace, in the words of the *Wrexham Advertiser* in July 1878:

> The [DRCR] was on Monday last, taken into the great system of the [LNWR], amid considerable rejoicings on the part of the Ruthin people, who have long believed that such an event would add greatly to their comfort and make their fortune. At 8.45 a.m. a train made up of five carriages all divided into compartments, and the 3rd class cushioned as all now are, started per time bill from Denbigh. On its arrival in Ruthin the drum and fife band were stationed in the yard, and [half of] Ruthin was down to see it, and there were great rejoicings. ... At 11.40 a new sensation was provided. Mr J. Guest, Mr E. Wood, District Superintendent, and several other officials from Chester rode over to inspect the line, they went in a special train of one composite

Ruthin station from the Denbigh direction in September 1961. It features an impressive brick-built engine shed, better than the one burnt down at Christmas 1875. **(WRRC)**

carriage, drawn by an immense engine with tender, and as they drew up at the stations the country people were somewhat amazed to see only one carriage, and that they were not allowed to go into it. [It was like the train on the Dee bridge picture at Corwen] The gentlemen alighted at each station, and took down particulars of what they saw, and gave instructions as needed to the stationmasters and others, and then shot off again on their mysterious journey.

But it was not all good news:

There is a manifest improvement [in comfort and speed], as everyone knowing the old third-class carriages and broken-down engines must see, but the service of trains is not better … There used to be a train at 2.55 and another at 3.55, but both are gone. Several other things occur equally inconvenient, while the only advantages reaped are improved carriages, and a late train from Corwen to Denbigh.

One advantage to passengers was the ability to travel from Corwen and Ruthin to Chester without changing trains. That happened because the LNWR controlled the MDJR alongside the DRCR, which it completely absorbed in October 1879.

The period of railway construction in north-east Wales from the early 1850s to the late 1860s saw competition between the LNWR and GWR that changed later into a joint effort by them to prevent an independent system of railways in Wales that challenged their domination. The LNWR aimed to prevent new railways and, if that failed, then to control them. The financial crash of 1866 put small Welsh railway companies in difficulty with two escape options – combine with each other and create a third force in Welsh railways or yield to the power and wealth of the LNWR. In practice, that power and wealth were so great, and the tactics of Euston so Machiavellian, that small lines had little chance to survive independently. So, the railways linked to the CHR were never as important as they could have been to the towns they served, and to Wales more generally, and when the rail system declined, they were the most vulnerable to closure.

Chapter 3

LNWR Flintshire and Denbighshire branches in action 1858-1923

Railways would do for [Welsh people] what nothing else would.
North Wales Chronicle
4 September 1869

Thus far we have examined the background to the growth of railways west of Mold that developed after the completion of the main line to Holyhead. We have seen that the LNWR outlined a policy that tolerated the creation of branch lines if local people funded them, and they presented no challenge to LNWR interests in north Wales. These tactics frustrated the development of a railway network that focused on the Welsh economy. Instead of the essential north to south connection, there was a series of low-powered branch lines in north Wales that served the main line on the north coast but did less than they might to develop the economy away from the coast. In this chapter we will look at the operation of the lines from Denbigh towards Rhyl, Mold, Chester and Corwen.

Construction of the VCR started in November 1857 at Fron Goed just to the north of the proposed station at Denbigh. At the other end of the line it was reported in February 1858 that a 'splendid new engine' was in use by contractors between Foryd and Rhuddlan. In March there was a heavy fall of snow that stopped the works, though it was reported that 'the contractors are pushing on the bridges and viaducts with great determination and rapidity', and that the new engine had replaced horse power in the cuttings and on embankments. The contractors aimed to open on 1 July, but after that date it was reported that 'ballast trains now run between Rhyl and St Asaph, [but from there] a good deal remains to be done [though] the very large embankment crossing Nant Patric (sic) and the viaducts on to Denbigh are nearly completed'.

The line eventually opened in October 1858, but hit its first snag in April 1859 with the question of running trains on Sunday. As the cathedral town of St Asaph had a station on the line, the directors initially organised trains that coincided with the times of Sunday worship, arguing that this was their purpose. This ruse did not fool the religious-minded and the directors dithered about continuing. One director saw it as no different from coal transport on a Sunday – 'a matter of £ s d, not a sabbath question' – while another thought that to 'desecrate the Sabbath [would] bring a frown upon our undertaking'. Timetables beyond the complete takeover of the line by the LNWR in 1868 continued to show no services on Sundays, even though connecting lines did have such services. I was unable to find exactly when Sunday services started between Rhyl and Denbigh, but it was later than most other lines in north Wales.

The VCR supported the 1860 national Eisteddfod at Denbigh with the 'utmost civility and attention to every grade of passenger'. Manager Martin Smith drew praise for his efficient management which contrasted with the shambolic VCR performance at the previous year's cattle show in Denbigh. Smith was a man with many duties on the railway. In 1863 he prosecuted Ellen Jones – 'a poor charwoman' – who had travelled with an invalid ticket. Smith agreed this was not a case for hard punishment, so a fine and costs of 1s 9d (£20) was imposed with a

The cathedral city of St Asaph was at the heart of argument about the morality of Sunday travel in 1859. By October 1966 passengers and such debates had long gone and the station appears to be a private dwelling. **(RCTS Photo Archive: collection of Jack Faithfull)**

week in jail in default. A year later he argued in Ruthin against the construction of waterworks and a market hall because the cost would fall in part on the railway as the largest ratepayer. That stance underlined the miserly LNWR approach to local economic development.

The early years of operation of the VCR had few incidents and accidents, in contrast to its volatile railway politics discussed in the last chapter. These were early days in railway operation, so employees and public took time to understand the sheer power and capacity for tragedy presented by railways. Events at St Asaph in June 1860 were a case in point:

> Two sets of points were left open, so that when the train from Denbigh approached the engine and guards van kept one line, while passenger carriages ran into a different siding, and were dragged from the line, much to the alarm and danger of the passengers.

Consistent with the custom of the day, the *North Wales Chronicle* knew who to blame:

> Great carelessness is attributable to some of the *subordinate officers* [my emphasis] and we are sure that the directors and secretary, who have ever been alive to the comfort and safety of the public will institute a minute enquiry into the matter.

That attentiveness from the directors did not extend to ensuring that a horse did not escape onto the track in the same week just north of St Asaph, putting the train at risk of falling down the embankment after the collision.

There was a more serious incident at Denbigh station in March 1861 when employee Edward Humphreys – a widower with three children – died during shunting operations. Such deaths were sadly common on railways for many years, and this incident exposed the general attitude towards them. Mr Gold Edwards, solicitor for the VCR, was at the inquest but need not have worried about the impact on the company after the coroner warned the jury not to be 'too apt find fault with a company or body of men' rather than focus on individual error. Humphreys was repairing a wagon between several other wagons when the engine shunted one of them too hard and trapped him. Conveniently, stationmaster Finlow told the court that he was about to report Humphreys for drunkenness when the death occurred and that was enough for the coroner to clear the VCR of all liability, noting only that it might have been a good idea to leave a little more space for Humphreys to carry out the repair the wagon. There was no mention of the fate of his orphaned children.

The rural nature of the line meant that animals were often more at risk than people. At Rhuddlan, two horses died under a train from Denbigh in 1882 as they crossed the line. Two carriages left the track, fortunately without injury to passengers, and the train went ahead with two coaches.

The construction of the DRCR was more complicated than the VCR, notably the Eyarth cutting and the bridge over the river to access Corwen. Its operation was also more challenging because of the severe money problems and changes in management. But it was the ever-active Martin Smith who featured once the Denbigh line reached Ruthin. Mr Dodson was stationmaster at Ruthin in 1864 and clashed with passenger Edward Evans, who taunted his Irishness and lauded the actions of local MP Williams-Wynn, commander of a force involved in the suppression of the Irish rebellion of 1798. Blows followed, and Smith arrested Evans at Denbigh with more fisticuffs. There were charges, counter charges, and great excitement in the vale before Evans's eventual conviction and fine.

Denbigh station had extensive sidings where Edward Humphreys met his death in 1861. A hundred years later the yard was still busy, though passenger services would soon cease. **(WRRC)**

Denbigh station was vital to its residents with its connections to Rhyl, Corwen and Mold, as reflected in this general photograph from 1906. (John Alsop Collection)

The poor state of the DRCR at this time emerged in a case against 11-year-old William Bundred in 1865. A train derailed after hitting a stone just south of the Eyarth cutting near to Pwllcallod farm where the lad was in service. He admitted to the police that he occasionally put small stones on the line to watch them crushed by the train but initially denied causing the derailment. The fact that the train was running 'tender-first,' that it had a history of derailment and that the crew had allowed it to run dry earlier in the day testified to the lax management of the line. But the critical evidence was that of the police officer who said Bundred had confessed on condition that the officer did not tell his father, at which Bundred blurted out, 'You promised to give me £5 (£500) and a suit of clothing.' The prosecution failed and the magistrate was critical of the engine running tender-first. Whatever the truth of the matter, the attitude of the court was not surprising because the chair of the bench was none other than Townshend Mainwaring, sometime chair of the VCR which at this time was in dispute with the with DRCR.

A similar incident at Corwen in February 1867 appeared to have more complicated origins:

> Considerable excitement was caused in Corwen Station on Monday evening, on the arrival of the 7.45 train from Denbigh, on it becoming known that a large stone had been mischievously placed on the Ruthin Line, just before the train reached the Iron Bridge ... Fortunately, the engine was slackening speed and the stone turned off without any further damage than breaking the engine – and a fright to the passengers. Much abhorrence of this attempt to run the train with its living cargo into the river was expressed, and the police and railway officials are using every means of bringing the villain to justice.

The company offered a reward, but the town stayed silent, and the *North Wales Chronicle* hinted at a reason for the attack on the line. The bridge replaced the site of a river ford and the railway company promised to replace this with a footbridge once the line opened but did not keep its word. It had then gone to great lengths to stop people using the railway bridge to cross the river, causing great local resentment.

But the hapless DRCR seemed more than capable of derailing its own trains as it did at Corwen in February 1870, reported by the *Aberystwyth Times*:

> The 8am train was observed crossing to the Llangollen line instead of proceeding on its own, and thus ran off the rails for about fifty yards; and if it had gone a few yards further it would have been over the embankment into the adjoining field ... but through the activity of Mr Buckton, Stationmaster, and Mr Livesey, of the locomotive department, sufficient hands were obtained to clear the way by noon. ... It is believed the points were out of order, or that some obstruction was between them, preventing their closing. ... The driver and stoker stuck to their post, and this was no doubt the means of stopping the engine and preventing a serious catastrophe.

Events such as these led one correspondent to call the DRCR 'one of the most peculiar lines in existence'. The context was a bizarre incident at Denbigh where a bull held in a pen killed a man after the railway company did not supply transport for the animal from the station and no other company would assist. The coroner summed up the state of railway relations at this time, this version from the *Wrexham Guardian* in April 1872:

> [At Denbigh] there were several companies' lines being worked [and] each company should assist the other in promoting the convenience of the public

at large. He was, however, sorry to say that this was not the case ... He hoped that before long the whole of these lines would be held by one company, and then they would see better regulations.

The fate of one engine, from the same newspaper in October 1875, showed the general state of the line:

> Travellers on the Ruthin line have become familiar with ... an engine called 'John Jones, Senior'. Often have we fretted and fumed in a railway carriage, despairing of being able to keep an appointment, because "John Jones", poor old fellow, had been suddenly seized with an attack of diarrhoea, asthma, or other internal malady, and must perforce stop midway probably between two stations, whilst his medical attendants ... operated upon him. What we believe will prove to be poor old John's death struggles, occurred on Saturday night. Employed to draw a passenger train from Ruthin to Denbigh, [he] was seized with a terrible fit on the incline near Brookhouse, [half a mile south-east of Denbigh station] and after struggling in vain, gave up in despair, and submitted to be drawn ... into Denbigh station, by a [LNWR] engine. [Later] taken to Ruthin, and consigned to the hospital, from which it is likely he will never emerge ... The decease of old friends is usually a matter of regret, but it seems hardly likely that any tears will be shed ... particularly as a fine new engine has taken his place.

A month later an insecure door caused a serious incident. When guard John Evans leaned out to speak to a driver of another train, he fell onto the line and was severely injured. The crew realised what had happened when the train reached Gwyddelwern from where it reversed, but GWR staff had already rescued Evans. A month later company staff celebrated the approach of Christmas by leaving a stove unattended in the wooden engine-shed at Ruthin. Fire destroyed the shed and tools, but the station survived, thanks to the vigilance of passing workers.

The optimism expressed at the arrival of a new engine in October 1875 was premature. In June 1877 there was evidence of failures to follow the block system on the line. A burst pipe stalled a train near Gwyddelwern, and its rescue took over three hours as the line had no electric telegraph, and the train continued, uncertain of when and where it would meet the other train and so 'it passed on to Rhewl, thence to Ruthin, Eyarth, Nant Clwyd, Derwen, to Gwyddelwern, with every possibility of a collision between each station ... the passengers who should have got to Denbigh at 4.10 arrived soon after seven'. No wonder there were such

Derwen station had little room for manoeuvre in the yard which led to the death of a carter in 1904 when an engine startled his horse. This photograph looking north in September 1961 captures the more typical rural tranquillity of the area. **(WRRC)**

celebrations when the LNWR took over, though it seemed that only then was old *John Jones*, along with the *Beeswing*, shipped off to Crewe for scrapping.

The wealth of the LNWR made a material difference to the operation of the line and the quality of its infrastructure but mishaps continued. In October 1885, horseboxes at Denbigh awaited coupling to the next train when the afternoon freight from Corwen descended too fast and smashed into them. There was extensive damage to the trains and an eight-hour delay to the 4pm train to Corwen. Fortunately the horse boxes were unoccupied. A horse at Llanrhaiadr did fall victim to the railway when it took fright at the arrival of the train and fell down a steep bank near the station sidings in 1891. The *Denbighshire Free Press* said

Gwyddelwern station saw drama in 1877 when a stalled train blocked traffic. This picture shows the station in 1961, eight years after closure to passengers. (WRRC) Inset: Ticket from Derwen from September 1946 as the LMS neared its end. (Michael Stewart Collection)

it was the third such event and complained that the LNWR took 'no steps to prevent any recurrence, by enlarging the goods siding and protecting the deep embankment [next to] the coal siding, and consequently [it was] highly dangerous alike to man and beast'.

Llanrhaiadr station experienced a series of mishaps towards the end of the nineteenth century. In 1906 it had a large staff and few passengers judging from this picture. (John Alsop Collection)

It was a similar story at Derwen station in 1904 where a cart load of timber fell on Ellis Jones who was trying to steady horses frightened by an approaching train. Again, the coroner noted the inadequacy of the siding arrangements, but he did not consider it relevant to the death of the carter. There was even greater cause for fright around Derwen with the arrival of a gas-filled balloon in the locality in October 1907, all the way from Battersea. The occupant could not make himself understood to local people who only spoke Welsh, and one young man was convinced that the end of the world had come with the descent of the Good Lord. After deflation, rail was the only way back to London, courtesy of station staff at Derwen who packed the balloon in a truck for its return from a record-breaking trip north.

Even the great LNWR could not prevent the actions induced by drunkenness, such as those of John Tudge and Richard Davies of Denbigh. They were close to the Llwyn Bach crossing south of the town. Tudge decided to use a platelayer's lorry to take his drunken friend home until crossing keeper Hannah Lloyd challenged them. She drove them off and removed the obstruction just before the arrival of a quarry train. Both men received six months hard labour.

More serious events occurred on the trains, as in February 1868 when Elizabeth Edwards, the wife of a Corwen jeweller, accused William Owen Jones, a Corwen solicitor's clerk, of a serious sexual assault when she was on the train between Ruthin and Corwen. Mrs Edwards said that she had treated the train guard to a glass of beer and offered two pence in return for him ensuring that she had a second-class compartment on her return. She said the guard asked her if she would accept Jones as a fellow passenger, to which she agreed.

The court heard also from the lamp cleaner at Corwen and from Robert Donald the DRCR railway police officer in charge of the time-interval railways signals at Corwen; he was also Mrs Edwards' lodger. The line's manager Cartwright explained the curious door locking procedures:

> The rule that the locks of doors on the offside … are to be locked [operates] on this line. [On market days] the doors which would be on the offside at the next stations would be locked. The locks are opened at Ruthin for Eyarth; they remain open for Nantclwyd … This is a single line, with stations on both sides of the line. When the train gets to Gwyddelwern, the side next to the station should be open.

The case went to Quarter Sessions at Ruthin in March 1868 where the judge favoured the defendant and excluded women from the court for the case. Later the railway line was the scene of strong feelings, according to the *North Wales Chronicle*, for and against the defendant in Corwen, when the decision of the jury to ignore the bill against Jones was known:

> When the 5pm train, which conveyed the complainant and her witnesses … arrived in the town the windows of nearly all the houses on the line … were occupied with females, who waved pocket handkerchiefs [expressing] their pleasure at the issue of the case. The next train … brought the defendant and his friends and it was [met] by a larger crowd [and he was] carried in triumph through the streets.

Later the same year there was an even greater show of public emotion at the arrival of Lord Napier at Rhewl station. He led an expedition to Abyssinia (Ethiopia) and rescued hostages at Magdala in July 1868, returning to Britain as a hero. He toured extensively and arrived at Rhewl station in October 1868. It was 'gaily decorated with flags and banners and evergreens, and in the chief streets of [Ruthin] triumphal arches were erected … one in the neighbourhood of the railway station, and one opposite the Town Hall.' Further homage was paid to the aristocracy at Nantclwyd station in 1885 when the inhabitants of the district gathered to greet Herbert Naylor-Leland of Nantclwyd Hall for his coming of age. 'On his appearing, he was received with much enthusiasm, and the horses were taken out of the carriage and, escorted by the Ruthin troop of Denbighshire Hussars … he was drawn by the tenants in triumph through the park.'

At the other end of the social scale was the fate of Daniel Roberts, a hawker living in the workhouse at Ruthin in 1895. He was an elderly man with no family and poor hearing. A train hit him near Ruthin station while he tried to cross the line, although the train crew noticed nothing, and it was children who had the misfortune to find the severely injured man who later died of shock at the station. Mr Carline of the LNWR was rather vague in response to a question about whether the company had sold grass cutting rights on the embankment to the deceased, but the jury accepted that Roberts had no right to be on the line and that his death was accidental. It congratulated a member of staff for applying a tourniquet to stop the bleeding, an early benefit from the LNWR's

Rhewl station gave a hero's welcome to Lord Napier in 1868 after his success in Abyssinia (Ethiopia). It closed to passengers in 1953 and ten years later was in poor repair. **(LNWR Society)**

Nantclwyd station welcomed aristocrat Herbert Naylor-Leland to public acclaim in 1885 on his coming of age but is noticeably quiet in this posed photo in the early 1900s. (WRRC)

introduction of first-aid training that had been highlighted at Denbigh station just four years earlier.

The MDJR was the first proposed extension of the LNWR system west of Mold but was the last of the major lines in this district. Construction was underway early in 1865 when many navvies struck after being required to work an extra half hour per day. They were back at work in the spring when a young Irish labourer died after being buried in an earth fall at Bodfari, while labourer Thomas Jones died nearby after jumping from a ballast wagon, though the coroner noted that timely medical intervention would have saved him. Work on the line then stopped due to the legal complications noted earlier but the company advertised for contractors in October 1868. The line carried coal earlier that year between Mold and Bodfari. Lillie Beeton stole some and the court sentenced her to seven days prison in June 1868.

The line opened in September 1869 and Martin Smith represented the LNWR – a man with a long history of managing railways in this region. His contribution to the proceedings was an example of the tension at the heart of railway development in north Wales. The LNWR worked hard to suppress the development of the Welsh amalgamation of which the MDJR was to be part, and Smith's comments, noted here in the *North Wales Chronicle* suggest more than a commercial motive:

> [Martin Smith] alluded to the great disadvantage which the Welsh laboured under in not being able to speak the English language. He himself should rejoice most to see the time when every portion of the Welsh people adopted the English language. (Loud cries of 'No, no', and 'Hear, hear') His friend on the left might not like it, but whether he did or not railways would tend very strongly to have it spoken in every part of Wales. ... He believed its [the Welsh language's] days were numbered, and the sooner the Welsh were truly and completely amalgamated ... the greater would be their prosperity; and on that ground he wished to see the English language universally spoken. (Applause from the upper end of the table, and dissent in the middle). Railways would do for them what nothing else would.

Unabashed by the controversial nature of his remarks, Smith wrote to the *Chronicle* reinforcing his sentiments:

> l recently recommended for employment fourteen Welshmen, well known to me as sober, industrious, and deserving men. It was necessary they should be able to read and understand a few plain instructions in English. Twelve altogether failed to pass; the remaining two satisfied the requirement, but only indifferently. This employment will go to Englishmen, or to Welshmen who happen to have learnt English, and who, consequently, possess the necessary qualification; but who are not in any other respect better men.

The context of Smith's comments is also interesting. In this district just three months previously there was fury among the Welsh population at the decision to sack a popular Welsh manager at Leeswood colliery and replace him with an Englishman who cut the wages. When the workforce struck there was a fierce response from the authorities and many arrests. As the convicted men were on their way from court to Mold railway station and jail in Chester, a riot erupted and there was an attempt to release the prisoners by the crowd. The army fired into the crowd around the station, killing four people. Smith must have known of the riot and was careless of the impact his statement might have in the district. Little had changed twenty-five years later when the LNWR dismissed Welsh employees for lack of English. The company was clearly happy with Smith's attitude and promoted him to District Goods Manager at Stafford in January 1871.

Smith's ambitions for local people to accept a loss of Welsh identity had negligible effect, judging by the response to efforts by bailiffs, police, and soldiers to secure payment of the hated tithes – a tax levied by the Church of England – at Bodfari station on the MDJR line in 1887, recounted here in the *Kentish Independent*:

> They were met by a crowd of several hundred persons, who prevented them [reaching a farm], and ultimately caused them to beat a hurried retreat to Denbigh. Here intelligence spread like wildfire that the bailiffs were in the town, and a crowd of the angriest character surrounded the place where they had obtained temporary shelter. Four of them eventually bolted for the railway station, and two ran down the railway for Ruthin, six miles distant, and were seen no more. The four men in the station were induced to come out, and when they did so were hooted, struck, hustled about and eventually flung bodily into the dirty water of an adjacent horse pond. They begged for mercy, and on promising never to come into Wales on a similar errand were allowed to leave the town.

Bodfari is quiet in this 1913 picture, but in 1887 saw a full-scale riot when the authorities arrived to distrain property for the hated tithe tax levied by the established church. **(John Alsop Collection)**

Denbigh had three lines after 1869, and by 1872 had fifty trains a day through its station including four goods trains. However, the old issue of using inadequate engines recurred with two broken down on the MDJR within a few days in November 1872, leading the *Llangollen Advertiser* to wonder whether 'the railway company work the Mold line with their old worn-out engines. It can scarcely be credited that they do'. While the engines were less than ideal, the drivers were occasionally obliging to the local population. A local blacksmith's daughter was ill at Denbigh and was married to Richard Jones, one of the MDJR drivers. The blacksmith jumped aboard his engine near Rhydymwyn to get news of his daughter and jumped off while the engine was moving, losing his life in the process.

A similar fate befell John Hughes, ex-porter at Nannerch station, who also wished to travel on an engine. He lost his life at Mold station amid the rowdy and drunken crowd joining the last Saturday train to Denbigh. He knew the engine driver and ran after the engine to jump aboard as it came into the station. He bumped into the crowd and fell under the wheels of the train. Mrs Duckworth of the King's Head agreed to allow him his final hours at her inn, but despite the views of the coroner's jury, the railway company declined to compensate her for her kindness. A young brakeman called Chambers was more fortunate and survived after being crushed between wagons at Caerwys a year later in the course of his duties. Thankfully there were no injuries when stones were placed on the rails near Nannerch – a surprisingly frequent occurrence more generally – in November 1906.

Nannerch station is attractive and well-kept in its prime. (John Alsop Collection)

After closure Nannerch was soon derelict and then disappeared under the realigned A541. (WRRC)

The oddest claim about the route between Denbigh and Chester occurred during a case against the former Kinnerton stationmaster William Hall in 1904. His ex-fiancée sued him for breach of promise when he cancelled their engagement. During the trial, Hall's representative maintained that his client's lack of poetry in his communications with Miss Davies was due to him being a stationmaster, most tellingly at Kinnerton, 'The dullest station in the world … where not a first-class ticket had ever been sold'. Hall progressed to Queensferry on the CHR by the time of the hearing in March 1904 and the court heard that he had greater prospects. The jury awarded £25 (£2,500) to Miss Davies.

The contrast with a nearby station could hardly be greater according to a report from a visitor in 1865. On arrival at Padeswood station, the 'oil prospector' considered himself to be somewhere like Canada or Pennsylvania such was the quality of what he found. In the event this 'discovery' proved as illusory as the

In 1904 Kinnerton was allegedly, 'the dullest station in the world' that 'never sold a first-class ticket'. This 1961 picture with inset shows such tickets existed – but not whether the railway sold any. (WRRC, Inset: Michael Stewart Collection)

earlier discovery of 'gold' that we noted near Denbigh. Hope station was also far from dull. Rioting miners captured it in 1863 during a dispute with the notorious Leeswood Colliery management and intended to despatch strike-breaking miners back to Wigan from the station.

The strangest fatality occurred at Rhydymwyn in 1878. Sarah and Thomas Griffiths were returning from Mold market to Rhydymwyn by the 5.30pm train and he was the worse for drink. They met Moses Jones and decided to stay on the train with him to Nannerch. Mr Griffiths changed his mind as the train was leaving Rhydymwyn and jumped on to the platform. His wife followed him despite efforts

Above: *Padeswood and Buckley station presents an impressive if faded spectacle as it approaches closure. It could all have been so different if the 1865 'discovery of oil' nearby had come to fruition.* (LNWR Society)

Below: *Rhydymwyn station in 1933. The level crossing gates where Sarah Griffiths died in 1878 are clear in this picture.* (John Alsop Collection)

Caerwys station near where authorities created a Territorial Army camp in 1910 and boosted business – but there is little activity in this picture from the early 1960s. **(WRRC)**

to stop her. She fell onto the level crossing gates, back under the train and died instantly. There was clearly no blame attached to the LNWR, though the jury still made the odd recommendation that the company should set the level crossing gates further back from the line, and also complimented passenger Jones for his efforts to save Mrs Griffiths despite the risk to his own life. The most remarkable survival was that of collier Meredith Jones who was walking on the line at Ffrith in 1906 when he was hit by a train and lost his arm. The injury involved twisting an artery which prevented heavy bleeding and enabled him to survive until found by the stationmaster next day.

The LNWR tended to contest any claim against it. When a local supplier of newspapers challenged the preference given to W.H. Smith at Denbigh station,

Ffrith station, where Meredith Jones narrowly escaped death in 1906, is behind the house on the right of this picture from 1995. The station closed in 1950 but the viaduct survived. (© Ben Brooksbank cc-by-sa/2.0)

he faced a stiff defence in court from the LNWR. He claimed that his case was 'really a fight for the trade of the town. We are newsagents and the defendants are common carriers ... bound to carry goods for everybody upon equal terms.' The company made clear that Smiths had 'special advantages' and the court agreed. Having won the case, the LNWR then secured costs against their opponent whose words echoed some local sentiment towards the company. 'You always fight every case, whether you are right or wrong.'

Businesses were conflicted in their attitude to the LNWR. They knew that the company had immense power and they had little influence in its direction. This was true of the MDJR that nominally remained independent up to 1923.

Year	Half year (£)	Total (£)	Adjusted to 2022 prices (£)
1882	3248	6496*	602338
1883	3484	6968*	653051
1884	3404	6808*	652079
1885	3476	6952*	688572
1886	3138	6276*	628761
1887	3338	6676*	676612
1888	3448	6896*	690876
1893	2998	5996*	593883
1894	3353	6706*	671941
1895	3082	6164*	624721
1898	3055	6110*	612130
1899	3162	6324*	626370
1902	3536	7072*	670003
1903	3758	7516*	704411
1904	3793	7586*	710971
1918		8605	376894
1920		8576	295451
1922		8559	374880

Table 2: Traffic receipts on the Mold and Denbigh Junction Railway for the years when data are available.

* Note: Data taken from newspaper reports are doubled to create the full year figure where only a half-year return was available.

That 'independence' enables us to gain an insight into business trends and the attitude of the LNWR to the traffic on its branches in Flintshire and Denbighshire.

Philip Pennant of Nantllys Hall, a member of one of the largest families in the Anglo-Welsh aristocracy, chaired the MDJR meetings in London. In November 1882 he noted that although they adjoined a mineral district, they were an agricultural line. Two years later he commented that trade in all sectors across the UK was 'very dull, in fact deadly dull'. He again emphasised agriculture as a factor and that Wales was cattle country, though the returns given at the meeting showed that livestock accounted for only 3 per cent of revenue. By 1888, the MDJR looked increasingly to minerals to improve its lot, but overall business improved only slightly.

By 1890 there was frustration among the directors, one of whom thought the MDJR was just a 'gathering ground' for the LNWR, and wondered if it could end the contract and compete with them or join others who were challenging the LNWR, a reference to the encroachment of Sir Edward Watkin's railways into north-east Wales. He thought progress was at 'a snail's pace which would not bring dividends for another half-century'. Pennant said it was hopeless to compete with the LNWR and they would receive poorer returns if they ended the contract, while suggesting that he had views on the Euston company that he would rather express in private!

By 1895 hopes were raised by the development of a brickworks and abattoir at Nannerch station. But business stayed flat and so a different approach was tried and the MDJR argued for a share of receipts at the two terminal stations on the line. The Railway Commissioners ruled the MDJR would only get the proportion represented by its mileage, meaning a loss of £127 (£13,817) in receipts rather than the increase of £100 (£10,879) that it claimed. In 1901, the chair accurately described the history of the line as 'one of slow, steady progress. There was nothing startling in it, but every year the line had a greater value than it possessed the year before'.

But there was a sense that the directors had had enough. In 1903, one shareholder asked 'whether any negotiations had taken place with the [LNWR] to buy the line. The Chairman said he preferred not to answer that question publicly; he would, answer it in private.' There was more bad news in 1904 with a report that 'there had been a decrease in the carriage of minerals, due partly to the mildness of the weather ... and also to the fact that the collieries had got into the bad habit of sending coal in motor wagons instead of by rail.' At least 1905 brought news of better train services, as 'a train now left London at 12.10 and arrived at Denbigh at 4.30 p.m. Another train did the journey up to London in about the same time.

Both were absolutely new trains, and, considering the distance was about 210 miles, this was pretty fair'.

Better trains brought more passengers by 1907 but 'to a certain extent the introduction of motors had decreased the first-class traffic'. The shadow of war brought extra traffic in 1910 when 'the Lancashire Territorial force encamped near Caerwys Station last August. The ground had been highly approved by the military authorities as a camping ground'. 1914 saw the opening the Star Crossing Halt and the introduction of a 'rail motor service' between Mold and Ruthin. The campaign for Star Crossing started in the 1890s, directed at the LNWR rather than the MDJR, showing that the independence of the latter was nominal.

Nonetheless, 1914 saw a significant attempt by the MDJR to hold the LNWR to account for its overall management of the line since the agreement of 1868. The legal case sheds light on the LNWR approach to branch line working in north Wales and its power over local interests. The MDJR complained that the LNWR breached the agreement of November 1868 by which it undertook to:

> Work, manage, maintain, renew, keep in order, and repair the railway works and junctions of the plaintiffs' line for the purposes of all traffic thereon, and were to work such traffic in a proper and safe manner, so as fully and in good faith to develop the traffic to be served by the applicants' railway.

Star Crossing opened in 1914 as the only new stop on the MDJR. The track and station look in good order in 1961 despite imminent closure to passengers. (LNWR Society)

Specifically, the MDJR alleged that the LNWR passenger trains were ill-timed, excursions were inadequate, local traders had insufficient trucks and sidings, troops for the camp at Caerwys went to Trefnant and Holywell rather than the nearer MDJR station, accounts of traffic on the line were inadequate and the LNWR sent goods and passenger over other routes even when the MDJR was the shortest route. The LNWR accepted that it worked the MDJR as if it were a branch line of its own and argued it had worked the traffic in the most convenient way, having regard to the facilities at its disposal. The MDJR considered that the LNWR had misconceived its obligations under the contract and it was bound 'to work and develop the applicants' line as if it were a separate and competing railway and were not entitled to treat it as a branch line of their own railway'. The court dismissed the case, concluding that the LNWR had wide discretion in working the line.

It is difficult not to sympathise with the MDJR. We have seen how it tried to join the amalgamation of smaller Welsh railways in the 1860s when LNWR control of Denbigh and Mold blocked its ambitions. Its only way out was to agree to the terms offered by the LNWR which, as the court showed in 1915, involved giving Euston a free hand in the use of the line. In the early days, there was enough money around for the LNWR to indulge the MDJR to some extent, but as the century progressed and railway finances tightened, so the LNWR had to make the most economical use of its infrastructure and the MDJR did not offer access to any location or source of the traffic that the LNWR could not tap by other means. The fate of the MDJR was exactly what Savin, Davies, Piercy, and France said it would be under LNWR control, like the outcome for most of the other branch lines in north Wales. In the period of the court judgement of 1915, the MDJR would eventually come under the control of the government like all railways in the First World War. In its final years of independence after 1919, the value of its traffic shrank in real terms, and it eventually disappeared as part of the London, Midland and Scottish Railway (LMS) in 1923.

There was one final challenge to the LNWR in north-east Wales that began at the end of the 1880s. Henry Robertson and Benjamin Piercy had continued with their interest in forging a specifically Welsh force in the railway world. That seemed to end dramatically in 1888 when both men died within a few months of each other. But there was a major political presence in the region, William Gladstone of Hawarden, who had been prime minister three times by 1888. Gladstone supported Henry Robertson and Benjamin Piercy's railway plans for the region to develop Aston Hall colliery that his family bought in 1885. When both Robertson and Piercy died Gladstone turned to Sir Edward Watkin of the Manchester,

This photograph at Trefnant in 1910 confirms the allegation in 1915 that the LNWR often used this rather than the MDJR station to serve the Caerwys army camp. (John Alsop Collection)

Sheffield and Lincolnshire Railway who was engaged in an ambitious challenge to companies such as the LNWR.

The issues for both crystallised into the single aim of giving Welsh traffic access to Liverpool via a new line from Wrexham over the river Dee north of Chester and under the Mersey. Both men exaggerated the benefits for north Wales by implying that such a line would challenge the wider LNWR monopoly in the region.

Gladstone dismissed companies such as the LNWR as being mostly concerned with long haul traffic and serving large cities. As the scheme progressed from the Mersey towards Wales and the vital bridge of over the Dee, Watkin explained to the 1888 Wrexham Eisteddfod mischievously that it was a 'gateway to Wales and hereafter *probably* to Ireland' (my emphasis) thereby raising Welsh hopes of breaking the LNWR monopoly in north Wales without promising to do so. Watkin also pointed out that railways in Wales were only 12 per cent of the total capital of the LNWR and GWR and clearly not their central concern. He hoped for Welsh railways paid for by Welsh finance and working for Welsh interests. It was a similar approach to Savin, Piercy, and Davies in the 1860s.

Watkin's efforts eventually produced the grand-sounding Welsh Railways Through Traffic Act 1889, which was an elaborate collaboration between small railways in Wales to create a through line between North and South Wales, and especially the coalfields, linking them to large markets in Lancashire and the port of Birkenhead. At least one optimistic Welsh commentator saw benefits for coal, tourism, agriculture and even a revival of Porth Dinllaen to challenge Holyhead. Its target was clearly the LNWR which according to one commentator unusually 'starves the victims it intends to devour', something that directors of the MDJR would have recognised. In practice, Gladstone's position was not substantially different from the earlier English railway promoters in Wales, as was clear when he opened the bridge over the Dee in 1889. 'They were all there ... gathered from different parts of England and formed into an army, and they had invaded Wales.'

Gladstone hoped to challenge the LNWR but on his death in 1898 he relied on it for his final journey to London starting on the Mold branch at Broughton Hall station in June 1898. In my history of the CHR, I incorrectly named the locomotive used for this journey. I am grateful to John Alsop for supplying evidence that the locomotive was a LNWR engine *Gladstone* from the Precedent class. The journey was the most famous, and most numerously observed, ever made on the branches and main line in north Wales. The point at which his funeral train joined the CHR was by the time of his death called Saltney Ferry, a change in 1891 when the station of that name opened. The Reverend Stephen Gladstone – the former PM's son – applauded the change and regarded the former name of Mold Junction as 'absurd'.

Briefly, there were high hopes from the Welsh railway legislation, with suggestions such as an extension of the MDJR to Abergele via St Asaph to challenge the congested CHR, and an extension of the Wrexham to Buckley line to the port of Mostyn via Northop, Halkyn and Holywell. More grandiosely, in 1896, aristocrat J.W. Wyatt of Bryn Gwynant Hall suggested a route from Watkin's line at Buckley through Mold, Ruthin, Cerrig-y-Drudion, Betws-y-Coed, Beddgelert, Porthmadog and on to Porth Dinllaen and he prompted an excited response and detailed map in the local paper with various senior figures in north Wales expressing support. But neither Watkin nor the LNWR were remotely interested, particularly as Wyatt suggested a monster tunnel under the mountains around Roman Bridge station. Captain Davies, the Harbour Master at Porth Dinllaen, was surely right when he said, 'His hair was now grey and would be black again before the scheme [to Porth Dinllaen] was carried out.' It was a rare prediction about railways in north Wales as it was correct.

It is possible that Wyatt's plan spooked the LNWR, because from around 1895 it increased capacity on the CHR by doubling much of the line from Chester to

Llandudno Junction to four tracks. It did so through the powers it obtained in the LNWR Act 1900 – though its work on the project started much earlier – including the use of stone taken from the Eyarth cutting in 1897.

There were other challenges to the LNWR. In 1909 there was a serious proposal for the Mid-Flintshire Light Railway linking Holywell with Mold. The LNWR response was rapid and by 1910 it was building a line from the main line at Greenfield up the steep bank to Holywell. It was not a straightforward process. In January, the construction staff put out a huge fire in Holywell and in February dealt with an elderly woman who refused to leave her home after the LNWR had purchased it.

Most seriously, in January 1912 a train with ten wagons loaded with construction debris left Holywell town for the tip at Greenfield with driver Samuel Bentley and two crew on the footplate. The brakes failed on the steep descent, the train gathered pace and smashed into the terminus near the main line, derailing the engine and the wagons and injuring the crew. The availability of trained first aiders, a motor ambulance, a local hospital, and a steam crane to recover the

Like Holywell, Prestatyn sprouted a short passenger branch with the opening of services to Dyserth in 1905. This picture from 1905 shows the primitive arrangements at Prestatyn with the unguarded main line to the right and the (now preserved) signal box behind. **(LNWR Society)**

wreckage were notable advances on the response when compared to earlier incidents noted in this chapter.

This line reversed the natural course of transport history because it involved the replacement of a motorised bus service by a railway. Holywell had been bypassed by the CHR but kept a connection through a haphazard horse and coach that the owner of the Kings Hotel upgraded. He became an agent for the LNWR until the company replaced his horse-drawn coaches with a petrol-engine bus in 1905. This late north Wales LNWR branch line may have been another effort to thwart competition consistent with company policy, but it was also an attempt to build better relations with local people as railways became more accountable to the public in the new century. The line had just one stop at St Winifride's, which turned out to be a popular attraction for those seeking a cure at the 'Lourdes of Wales', prompting one speaker at the opening ceremony to suggest 'Health, Holiness and Hill Walking' as the slogan for the line.

This was a correct assessment, with one mass visit of Catholic pilgrims from the Midlands in 1913 attracting 800 people on two trains. The LNWR associated closely with the Church of England but a search for profit was always a priority at Euston so Catholic custom was welcome. A pilgrimage of a different kind, with echoes of the modern era, occurred in November 1914 when refugees from

St Winifride's was the one stop on the Holywell branch and served the religious 'Lourdes of Wales', though the factory smoke shows that God and mammon were side by side. (John Alsop Collection)

Above: *The Holywell Town station was in a hollow close to the town. The large crowd and bunting are to celebrate the opening of the line in 1912. (John Alsop Collection)*

Below: *LNWR staff stand proudly next to a Dyserth rail motor which served the public well until 1914, after which reliability became more of a problem. (John Alsop Collection)*

Belgium arrived at Holywell Town station fleeing the conflict at home only to find that no arrangements existed, and they had to go to nearby Greenfield.

Before the Holywell development, the LNWR had added passenger services to the Prestatyn to Dyserth line in 1905. Contractors Scott and Edwards completed the line in 1869 but the LNWR used it for mineral transport until the public demanded passenger services. In June 1905, locals noted 'large gangs of men employed relaying the metals', and rumours were printed in the *Prestatyn Weekly* that '… upwards of 100 men are coming, or have come, to relay the permanent way on the Dyserth line [meaning] nothing less than an early commencement of passenger traffic'. They were right, and there were intermediate stations provided at Chapel Street, Rhuddlan Road (Woodland Park from 1923) and Meliden. There was clearly a commercial value in the service as a year later the *Rhyl Record* told its readers:

> The facilities offered by the motor train for exploring the lovely countryside in the neighbourhood of Dyserth are being taken full advantage of by the visitors at Rhyl and Prestatyn … the number of passengers swollen [so much] it is the intention of the [LNWR] to run … 28 journeys daily.'

This increase in traffic on a line that was already well used by goods trains caused some difficulty, reported here by the *Prestatyn Weekly*:

> In consequence of the frequent journeys of the passenger car, the goods train which once a day ascends the line to Dyserth is now obliged to perform its journey in the early hours of the morning. To-day (Friday) the goods train by some unexplained reason crashed into the stop-block placed at the end of the line at Ochr-y-Foel, damaging both the permanent way and the guard's van. It is stated that several men have been injured in consequence of the mishap.

Local people requested improvements and in 1908 the same newspaper noted that 'Lord Stalbridge [LNWR Chair] considers Meliden as one of the great cities of the future. The station box [shelter] has already arrived. Joking apart, this will be a convenience to passengers who in wet and stormy weather sometimes have to wait the arrival of the motor train.'

The LNWR planned to extend the line to Newmarket, but the plan needed a road bridge costing £2,500 (£248,000) for which the LNWR would not pay. When the Railway Commissioners agreed the need for a bridge, the company offered £350 (£35,000) towards it but that was insufficient and although work began (still visible in 2022 near Marian Mill) the LNWR did not complete the line.

William Gladstone and Sir Edward Watkin aimed to challenge the LNWR monopoly in north-east Wales by connecting the region with Liverpool and Birkenhead using a bridge over the River Dee near Shotton – seen here just ahead of this Wrexham bound Class 150 in 2015. **(Phil Lloyd Collection)**

The failure of this extension was a minor matter compared to the lack of success with larger proposed routes within the LNWR sphere of influence. A major failure was the Ruthin to Cerrig-y-Drudion railway which local landowners, including Townshend Mainwaring of the VCR, supported from 1876. The line received Royal Assent in July 1876 to the accompaniment of the church bells at Ruthin; and by September contractors had marked out the route. By November, the Town Crier at Ruthin tried to garner public support and optimism persisted but without tangible results. In 1878, local hopes focused on the LNWR, though it is difficult to see what advantage the line offered to Euston, even if connected with Betws-y-Coed as some suggested.

In October 1878, the line was only £6,500 (£640,000) short of the amount required by the contractor to build it. But an appeal to local businesses failed to deliver the money. By February 1879, a St David's Day ceremony was planned for cutting the first sod, but in May Mrs Sackville-West offered to return to Ruthin, 'for whenever the-much-put-off ceremony was fixed'. Ominously, the ceremony was abandoned even though around a mile of track was constructed from Ruthin by June 1879. According to the *Carnarvon and Denbigh Herald* in September, the project descended into farce:

> A few months ago, after great difficulties in getting the capital subscribed had been overcome, a narrow guage (sic) railway … was commenced. Only about three miles has been cut, and now a large number of the shareholders … have refused to pay the calls made upon them. A number of them were summoned to the county court for this week … Difficulties have also arisen with the labourers and gangers employed. The shareholders allege that the agreement as to the cost of the line is not being adhered to, hence their refusal to subscribe more capital.

By November, the works had stopped, and the future of the line switched to the courts. In February 1880, the directors consulted Henry Robertson, the notable railway developer, who suggested engineer Henry Jackson had made unwarranted claims of £8,000 (£796,000) including claiming for 13,000 yards of rock cutting while Robertson found only 580. The company secured permission from parliament to abandon the scheme in 1884. Thirty years later, the LNWR, having stayed clear of the discussion about a railway, agreed to supply a bus service between Mold, Ruthin and Cerrig-y-Drudion. But the ill-fated connection between these towns failed again as the manufacturer did not deliver the vehicle. War broke out a few days later and it is unclear whether the LNWR ever delivered a service.

There is a final significant incident to note in the operation of railways in Flintshire and Denbighshire before 1923 – the national strike of 1911. This was a fierce dispute with local hero David Lloyd George trying to negotiate a settlement. The reaction to the strike in Denbigh shows how essential the railway was to rural Wales at this time, reported by the *Denbighshire Free Press*:

> Denbigh people, who are absolutely dependent on the [LNWR] for locomotion were gratified to find that the different grades of railway men at Denbigh, almost to a man remained absolutely loyal to their company and continued at their work in the passenger and goods departments running the trains and attending to the passengers and traffic, notwithstanding a good deal of pressure to come out. … Consequently, little or no inconvenience was experienced on this section [involving] the trains through from Corwen and Denbigh to Chester via Mold and from Chester via Rhyl to Denbigh. [The staff] were subjected to violence, stones and other missile being thrown

especially at Mold – in addition to the "peaceful picketing" which was the vey reverse of peaceful in many cases.

The dispute was the focus of religious services with prayers for its resolution: 'In St Mary's Church an extremely appropriate sermon was preached … the rector expressed thankfulness … that the sad dispute had practically ended.' The LNWR posted its own message that showed little inclination to compromise with the strikers and ordered that: 'Double pay is to be given for the period of the strike to all those men connected with the movement and handling of traffic who have remained loyal.'

The conduct of the strike in this area of north Wales showed the power of the LNWR over its workforce. Railway work was not well paid, was dangerous and exhausting but it was regular and dependable at a time of great financial hardship. Although the strike was over, the international strife was just beginning and would explode into worldwide war and control of the railways by the government which the LNWR would only briefly survive.

The most significant contribution to the war effort in this area was the completion of the railway link from the ever-growing Kinmel Park military camp to Rhyl via the VCR at Foryd. It opened with great ceremony in June 1917, described by the *North Wales Chronicle*:

> The journey takes on an average 20 minutes, and … the [LNWR] have given the military authorities every help in carrying out the necessary arrangements. … [The] opening ceremony was performed by General Sir Pitcairn Campbell [and] a large company were entertained to luncheon … A train … decorated with the colours of the Allies … slowly approached the platform … amid a hearty cheer from those present … A half-holiday was given the troops, who were also granted free travelling facilities for the occasion.

The process of completing the railway system in Flintshire and Denbighshire finished by 1900, with the small branches to Dyserth and Holywell something of a footnote. The other exception was Sir Edward Watkin and the North Wales and Liverpool Railway. It had William Gladstone's support and succeeded in linking Wrexham and Deeside to Liverpool, thus avoiding the need to go through the LNWR/GWR citadel of Chester General Station. The wider plans of Watkin and Gladstone to extend westwards from the Dee, if they ever existed, got nowhere. Instead, the LNWR power in north Wales appeared to be on an endlessly upward trajectory. But eventually the petrol engine, replaced by a train on the short branch to Holywell, returned decisively.

Chapter 4
The Eastern Slate District

> To attempt, to work this line [to Llanrwst] without the co-operation and good will of the [LNWR] – or, rather against their consent, would have been a somewhat dangerous experiment.
>
> *North Wales Chronicle,* 1863

In this chapter we move west from the fiercely contested areas of Flintshire and Denbighshire to consider the development of railways that snaked along the valleys to the slate districts of Blaenau Ffestiniog and Bethesda. Competition with the GWR was not a feature here to the same extent, and the proponents of a third railway force in Wales were also not so active. Nonetheless, the LNWR was determined to keep tight control of railway development and used the same process of opposition, disruption, and inducement to secure its power in the region. The development of railways in these districts occurred simultaneously with those discussed in earlier chapters and the results were broadly similar – a relentless process of acquisition by the LNWR and a significant lack of a strategic approach to the use of railways to develop the economy of north Wales.

The earliest interest in branch development west of Abergele was the short line to Llandudno from the main line at what is now Llandudno Junction. This development was no surprise because the St George's Harbour Railway had been a potential rival to the CHR as early as 1836 when its proponents argued that ending the line from Chester at modern day Llandudno would save the cost of crossing the river at Conwy and the Menai Straits, thereby compensating for the added time taken to sail from Llandudno to Dublin. The various reports commissioned by government did not support that argument and the scheme disappeared.

However, the skilful and far-sighted development of Llandudno by the Mostyn family from 1849 revived the case for a railway, as did the hazardous experience of travelling by horse drawn bus to the town. In September 1857, a bus that had picked up passengers at Conwy station overturned on the road to Llandudno killing the driver and injuring passengers. The poor state of the vehicle and the road caused the accident, which was the sixth in a year. So the need for a railway was clear but the process not so simple. The original St George's Harbour Railway

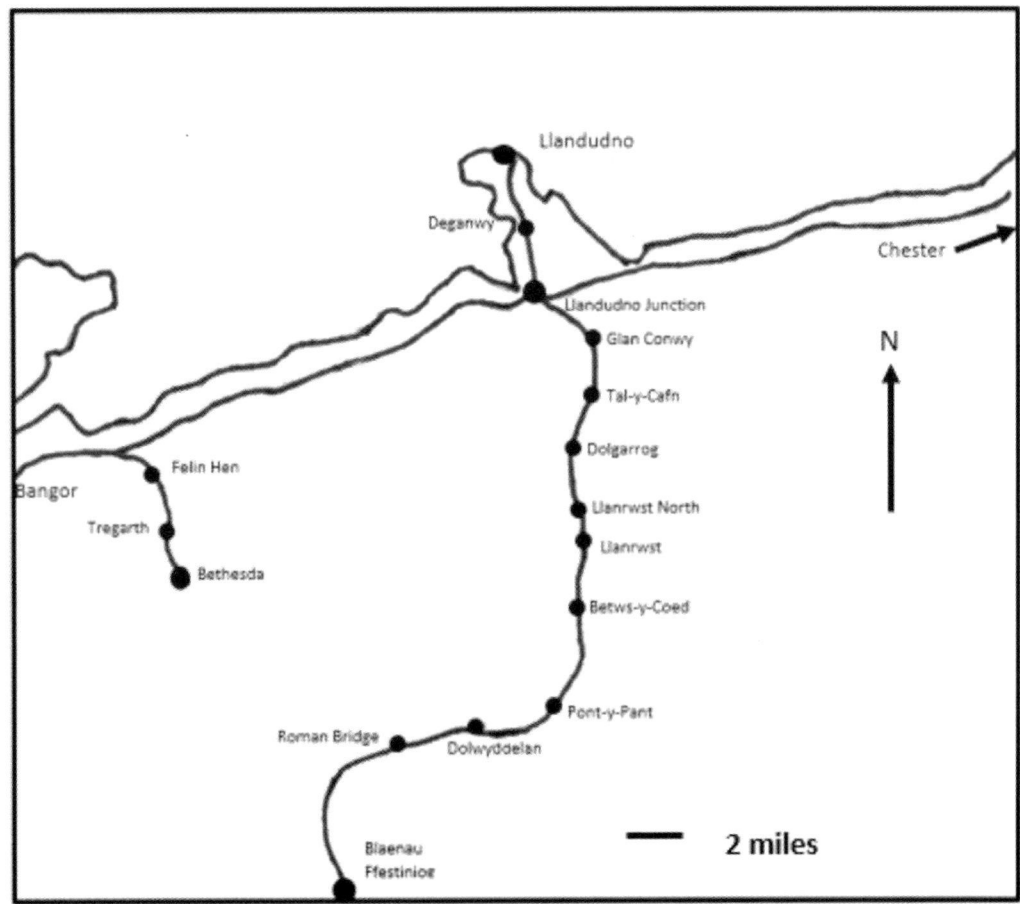

Map 3: The Eastern Slate District: LNWR branch line stations c 1918.

Act of 1853 required it to build a pier and harbour before the railway. A later amendment relieved the company of this obligation, and it abandoned its original scheme to tunnel through the Great Orme in favour of a pier nearer to the town. Parliament refused the right to build a station on the seafront because it limited access to the beach.

In July 1858, the line progressed rapidly with a junction at 'Conway Ferry' planned to allow trains to go directly to Llandudno from the east without calling at Conwy. There was no formal opening but in September 1858 the area experienced 'much excitement and joy … when the engine passed on the railway from the ferry junction to Llandudno for the first time'. In October, according to the *Daily News*, 'The first train started from Llandudno at 8.35 am and completed the journey in something less than 10 minutes. Eight passenger trains are to run daily to and from, and arrangements have been made ... for through carriages from Birmingham, Liverpool, Manchester, and London.'

But as was usual with railway projects, early joy preceded disappointment and demands for improvements. In August 1862, the local commissioners in Llandudno tackled the LNWR about the state of the pier, which Euston accepted was its responsibility as it had by then absorbed the line. By November, the complaints from the town had turned to the subject of motive power on the branch line. The *North Wales Chronicle* shared its readers' feelings. 'The utter contempt with which the LNWR treat the inhabitants of this place is beyond anything ever heard of ... they have now added injury to insult by substituting horse for locomotive power along this small branch [in winter].'

Two years later the LNWR supplied steam traction all year round but, as on other branches further east, the quality was not the best. One correspondent to the *North Wales Chronicle* noted that the 9.40am train from the junction took 45 minutes to reach Llandudno, apparently a common occurrence. The state of the terminus at Llandudno was a consistent source of complaint, described as 'an eyesore and crying evil to all persons ... on account of its shabby architecture, in comparison with our otherwise splendidly built town'. In 1869 the LNWR relented and committed money for improvements. It went one better in 1892 and provided £30,000 [£3.2 million] to complete a new station.

In 1892 the LNWR built a station at Llandudno that matched the scale of the tourist traffic. Remarkably, it was not until 1904, the date of this picture, that trains served the town on Sundays. (John Alsop Collection)

There were regular complaints about tourist rowdiness in Llandudno. It is unlikely the Fletcher Street Methodist Choir seen at the station in 1900 were a problem. (John Alsop Collection)

There were few accidents and incidents on the line though 'a considerable portion … was washed away by the furious tide' in January 1863. Derailment caused loss of track in January 1866 when:

> The 6.30am train to the Junction was passing Towyn [and] the engine went off the rails [it tore] up the line for a score of yards turned over and buried itself in the sand. The first of the three carriages went off the line… but came to a stop with the others before much damage was done … Driver John Pugh, one of the company's most careful and intelligent servants, was the only person injured.

It took a day to fix the line during which passengers and parcels experienced an early version of the rail replacement bus.

The level crossing at Deganwy where two SS Avenel *sailors died in 1901. The quay where they docked is to the right of this photo from 1909. (John Alsop Collection)*

Events at Deganwy station in November 1901 were far more serious. By then the LNWR had constructed a large quay there for the export of slate, also used by other ships including the SS *Avenel* which was unloading cement. William Miller and John Murphy went into town in the evening for a drink and platelayer Lewis Roberts discovered them by on the track next morning after a train killed them on the level crossing. The *Avenel* did not survive much longer, wrecked at Thurso in January 1906.

A year after this incident, two trains waited to leave Llandudno station, but the Holyhead express wrongly responded to the clear signal intended for a local freight. Signallers directed the train at high speed into a siding near Maesdu where it smashed into the buffers, fortunately causing no serious injuries.

Although technically a branch line, the route to Llandudno was really an extension of the main line to carry vast numbers of tourists to its terminus. While that was a benefit to the town, there was occasionally a downside as in July 1890 when the *North Wales Chronicle* reported that 'there were scores of drunken men rolling about the streets at nine o'clock in the morning [using] the most disgraceful language. [Apparently] there was a promise from the [LNWR] that they would not bring more than a thousand excursionists per day [but] there were about 8000 last Monday.'

By contrast, Sundays were quiet as late as 1904, according to the *Rhyl Journal*:

> Incredible as it is, there is a large and influential number of persons who object to trains being run on Sundays, and they are going to 'depute' the Town Council in opposition. Llandudno is some miles at present from a Sunday stopping train and there is much driving back and fore. The good people referred to prefer all this bustle to that of a few minutes at the railway station two or three times a day.

Nonetheless the Sunday service began that summer with three trains a day in each direction.

The pressure on the railway from high tourist numbers sometimes had profound consequences such as the death of John Astin of Brighouse in 1905. He was returning with the Blakeborough and Sons valve works outing and standing with a large crowd as the train arrived. In the rush for the carriages, he fell off the platform and under the train with fatal consequences. Three years later, one of the 2,000 employees of Gossage's Soap Works who visited Llandudno from Widnes on a day trip fell off the platform as a train arrived, but the guard's rapid use of the vacuum brake saved him.

As the end of the century approached, the crowds at Llandudno were increasingly swelled by soldiers who attended camps along the north Wales coast. They tended to arrive in the town by boat and then either march to camp or take a train, particularly as the camp at Conwy Morfa had its own station from 1894. The soldiers attracted attention, as reported here by the *Carnarvon and Denbigh Herald*, particularly during the patriotic fervour of the Boer War in June 1900:

> There was a scene of wild excitement at the railway station on Saturday night, when the Lancashire soldiers finally departed, the camp on Conway Marsh [Morfa] being struck on the following day. The men had spent their last evening in Llandudno and ... about three hundred marched to the station to catch the last train, which was somewhat late, and so they whiled away the time with songs. The station does not make a bad impromptu music hall, and to the few spectators present at that late hour (10.30) the proceedings were highly diverting.

The First World War brought an even greater level of military activity with various units based along this short branch. The railway contributed its share of recruits, mostly from clerical staff. A meeting in Llandudno in 1917 heard that one in ten of the 80,000 railway clerks in the UK were in the forces. The railway company often then employed women for these tasks. Of the men who went to war, at least one local recruit died in action. Gunner Jesse Ayres, of the Royal Field Artillery, who served in the office at Llandudno for eight years, died in June 1917

The end of the war brought peace abroad but industrial problems at home. A major rail strike in 1919 showed how vital the railways were to community life. News of the end of the strike caused a huge demonstration of public relief at Llandudno Junction with prayers said and hymns sung, just as we noticed at Denbigh at the end of the 1911 strike. Managers had arranged to operate a skeleton service with a motor train between Llandudno and the junction run by them if the strike continued. The authorities in Llandudno were frustrated by the strike and drew 'attention to the great expense, inconvenience and discomfort caused to Llandudno visitors by being compelled to go by road'. It would not be too long before they would be demanding more not fewer road facilities!

The creation of the Llandudno branch raised the issue of its extension south along the Conwy valley. We noted in Chapter 1 that Edmund Sharpe advocated a narrow-gauge line on the west side of the valley from Llanrwst to Conwy in 1857, with a tramway south from Llanrwst to Betws-y-Coed. In July 1858, as the Llandudno branch neared completion, there was a large public gathering in Llanrwst Town Hall, chaired by Henry Robertson Sandbach, a prominent local landowner. He reviewed the earlier efforts to secure a line, backed Sharpe's proposal and emphasised the importance of securing private not public investment, a curious position to adopt by a man whose family wealth at that time derived in part from the £130,000 (£15million) of public money given in compensation for the loss of his slaves in Guiana.

Sandbach may have been aware of the comments made at the CHR shareholder meeting in March 1858 which heard that 'with regard to the Conway Valley line, the company had no idea of subscribing one shilling towards [it], although they would be happy to accommodate the traffic and to see the line made'. Sharpe reiterated his views on the advantages of the west bank scheme but offered the prospect of a change to the route north from Tal-y-Cafn, where the line could switch to the east of the river. Doubtless he did so because of the construction of the Llandudno branch and its junction with the CHR on the east of the river Conwy. Oddly, he continued to argue for a 39 inch gauge.

The most significant intervention was from James Bird, an experienced railway investor, who 'had come expressly … 250 miles to attend this meeting [but] his interest lay at the other end of the line [and he thought] it was of the utmost importance that they should secure facility of access across the [CHR] into the Llandudno branch'. He based his argument on the poor facilities for carrying slate by road and water from Blaenau Ffestiniog that a railway to a terminal port could replace, and he revealed that he had already bought land for a slate wharf at Deganwy.

Bird's knowledge of the methods of the LNWR was clear in his next assertion that a line on the east side of the river would be attractive to Euston because it would remove the risk of the GWR 'who were on the lookout for an opportunity to raise a line across the country to this part, so as to compete with the [CHR] in the Irish traffic.' That shifted Sharpe who saw 'the absolute necessity … to give no umbrage' to the LNWR. Bird then offered to supply a significant investment for a scheme that met his requirements.

In November 1859, proposals appeared in the press that conformed to those requirements and included an extension to Betws-y-Coed. Hanmer of Bodnod (now Bodnant) cut the first sod at Maenan Abbey in September 1860, by which time Edmund Sharpe was chair of the company. However, progress was slow: so slow that it was not until January 1862 that the Llanrwst Eisteddfod could award a prize for the best poem 'in praise of [Sharpe] through whose never-to-be-enough praised exertions a railway has at length been set on foot'.

The construction of the line went ahead smoothly, consistent with the level route and limited need for rock cutting and tunnelling. In May 1863, the contractors held a celebratory event at the Erskine Arms in Conwy for their staff. It was notable for the absence of any local worthies and for the praise heaped on Edmund Sharpe and the ever-popular LNWR district manager Hedworth Lee.

The formal opening of the Conwy and Llanrwst Railway was a much grander affair a month later. The notes of the proceedings show that the LNWR (through Hedworth Lee) supervised construction, and there was never any doubt (unlike some lines further east) that it would become part of the Euston empire on completion. The line had three stations: Llansanffraid (renamed Glan Conway in 1865); Tal-y-Cafn; and Llanrwst, where the LNWR sited the station to suit local landowners rather than the townspeople.

The line's low cost of £60,000 (£6.2million) for 12 miles was a measure of the ease of construction. A train full of guests left Manchester Victoria station at 8am on 16 June 1863, and arrived at Llanrwst at 1.30pm for the banquet at the Eagles Hotel, showing that city as important for the finance for the scheme.

The proceedings revealed the deliberate challenge to Welsh culture in this development. Colonel (later Sir) Arthur Bigge, a military man and eventually secretary to Edward VII, remarked that 'the Saxons had made very great inroads into Wales. They were there that day to celebrate the last of these … and that was the formation of the system of railroad into Llanrwst'. It was a theme picked up by the vicar of Conwy who thought this conquest of Wales had been 'carried by no … angry clash of hostile hosts [but had] made a breach whereby Saxon youth may poise their lances before Celtic beauty'.

Hardman Earle, a director of the LNWR, seemed to understand the ambivalent nature of local feeling towards his company and the *North Wales Chronicle* shared his words:

> It was true they were accused of a grasping policy in extending their lines in all directions, but the neighbourhood of Llanrwst could not complain, for by subsidising, making and buying lines the [LNWR] had opened up a series of branches to all parts of [north Wales] that had amply compensated the company.

Earle was a senior director on the LNWR and gave his name to Earlestown, the junction between the LMR and the GJR. He also knew a bit about compensation as, like Henry Sandbach, the government had compensated his family as former slave owners in 1838.

Sharpe did not stay around long to check on progress. Local worthies treated him to a dinner three months after the line opened, after which he left with his profits for Geneva, from where he undertook further railway ventures including a line from Geneva to Carouge. His comments at the latter dinner (reported by the *North Wales Chronicle*) provided unmistakable evidence of the balance of railway power in north Wales and why his original narrow-gauge plans had not survived:

> [I cannot] complain of the course which [LNWR] thought it necessary to pursue in requiring me to part with the possession of the property to them. For no one who takes up a map of this part of the country can fail to observe that the continuation of this line to Corwen would open to others [the GWR] as ready an access to Llandudno and the Irish Sea, as is at present enjoyed by the [LNWR] alone … I was, also, perfectly aware that to attempt to work this line as I had hoped, in connection with, and in continuation of, the Llandudno Railway, without the co-operation and good will of the [LNWR] or, rather, against their consent, would have been a somewhat dangerous experiment.

The line was soon the scene of an unusual accident in July 1864. Richard Jones worked on the railway and took his sister and others to a show at Llansanffraid by train. He waited for the last train to Llanrwst to pass and then stole a platelayers' lorry to take the group home, assuming that there would be no more trains. However, a light engine on its way to Bangor for repair hit the lorry near Tal-y-Cafn, killing Margaret Jones. At the chaotic coroner's inquest, many jury members could not speak English – the language of all legal processes in Wales even when not spoken locally – and there was a strong feeling that the court should not blame Jones. The coroner spelled out the process of following evidence and the law, but the jury returned an accidental death verdict, despite the coroner insisting it was manslaughter. A death at Llanrwst station in 1867 was less controversial. Staff advised a man against unloading heavy timber in the station yard, but he persisted and died when the load fell on him.

Local hopes of the value of the new ownership expressed by Sharpe and others when the line opened faded when the LNWR extended it to Betws-y-Coed. Construction started in August 1866 and ended in September 1867, meeting

Tal-y-Cafn station saw more than its share of serious incidents. This picture is from BR days when all was calm, and the station still had gas lights. **(WRRC)**

few difficulties apart from a dispute with the owner of Berth Ddu farm, south of Llanrwst. He claimed the railway prevented his cows accessing the river because of its 'smoky, screaming embankment'. The LNWR eventually agreed compensation.

'A RESIDENT' explained local disappointment with the LNWR in the *North Wales Chronicle* in November 1867, echoing the more general sentiments about its operation of branch lines:

> Loud is the complaint of those living in the neighbourhood of this railway, against the parsimony of the [LNWR], in delaying to open the line. This railway was completed about two months ago, and it is now reported that no passengers will be conveyed by it until the spring, for no other reason than the smallness of the profit likely to be realized by the [LNWR]. This niggardly mode of proceeding is unworthy of a great company. When the bill received the sanction of parliament, and landowners were forced to sell their property, it was supposed that the accommodation of the public required such a sacrifice; but what does the conduct of this company indicate? Clearly that the only consideration to be thought of is their own interest. The convenience and comfort of the people living in the neighbourhood, and through whose land the line passes are ignored, and the large returns expected from the summer excursionists and tourists (the terrors of quiet people) are alone regarded.'

Betws-y-Coed station hosted an eisteddfod in its warehouse in January 1868 and there was a report of the line opening on 6 April and that 'it was a rather expensive undertaking, there being several bridges and deep cuttings. [The opening] was allowed to pass without any demonstration.' Construction produced at least one casualty, an unnamed labourer from Anglesey buried by an earth fall in the cutting at Cwmlanerch. In January 1869, the river washed the line away between Llanrwst and Tal-y-Cafn and a train plunged into the river with no human casualties. Seven unfortunate pigs drowned and were 'soon converted into innocent bacon'. The battle with the river was to be a constant theme on this line. Nonetheless, the LNWR sought powers to extend it to Blaenau Ffestiniog in 1871, despite a general feeling that the undertaking was too expensive to contemplate. Unusually for the LNWR, it initially planned a narrow-gauge extension from Betws-y-Coed.

Reaching Blaenau Ffestiniog proved to be a longer process and involved a project that almost matched crossing the Menai Straits in 1848–50. There was little activity on the new line after the first statement, but the move by the GWR to access slate at Ffestiniog with a line from Bala spurred the LNWR, which objected strongly to the GWR plans. Euston hurriedly planned a line, secured

Betws-y-Coed station had a heavy tourist traffic and featured a substantial goods yard to the right in 1903, used for an eisteddfod in 1868. **(WRRC)**

parliamentary approval, and started construction in 1874 under the direction of its own engineering department.

The scale of the tunnel into the terminus attracted widespread interest. The North Staffordshire Society of Mining and Mechanical Engineers examined the works in 1876 and supplied an illuminating account:

> The tunnel [will] when completed, be two miles and a quarter long. About four hundred men are now employed ... The tunnel is being pierced from both ends, three shafts have been sunk [and] six other faces are being simultaneously worked. The mud and debris are raised through the shafts by means of cages, to which are attached safety hooks for the prevention of accident in case of overwinding. ... The rock drilling machines in use are of three kinds, the Burleigh, the McKean, and the Ingersoll ... worked by compressed air ... The ventilation of all the workings is perfect, the

compressed air effectually accomplishing this after exhaustion from the drilling machines. The compound used for blasting is cotton gunpowder, or guncotton, [very safe] except when ignited by a detonator [but see below].

The tunnel at the north end is now opened out to its full area to a depth of about 180 yards, and the nature of the rock at this part is such that no lining of brickwork will be required. From the south end of the shafts only a small heading is first driven, in order that when opening the tunnel to the full area the debris may be conveyed away by means of a tramway, instead of the more expensive method of raising it up the shafts. ... Some idea of the expenses ... may be gathered from the fact that before any material progress could be made with it, a circuitous road some three miles in length had to be constructed up the mountains, for the conveyance of plant, materials, and coal, for use at the shafts, and in the operations beneath.

Four 'barracks' have also been erected at remote parts of the line, which are capable of accommodating sixty or seventy workmen. Mr Roston, foreman of the mechanics, has also erected at one of the shafts, premises equal to a small factory, in which are appliances for repairing machinery. The line at Festiniog when completed will be at an elevation of about 700 feet above the level of the junction at its commencement.

The tunnel proved costly, accounting for half the total £500,000 (£51.4million) price of the line. The human cost was high too. In July 1876, Henry Davies was preparing explosives for blasting in Shaft 3 when the charges ignited before expected and wounded him fatally, a fact obviously not mentioned to the visitors from Staffordshire a week later. In September 1876 there were reports of construction workers using tunnel-drilling machines instead of explosives. The rock was so hard that sometimes only 30ft per week were completed, although at that stage 1,000yds had been cut and blasted and it was predicted to take a further two years to complete. Mr Roston, mentioned in the report above, lost his son who fell from a moving engine and was crushed under its wheels north of the tunnel in June 1877. This was also the month when the GWR confirmed that it would build its line from Bala to Blaenau Ffestiniog, so the LNWR was ahead of its rival.

The tunnel opened in July 1879 but the most serious incident occurred early in that month. William Hughes, George Carroll, and John Jones died on 3 July after a train hit their pedal-operated platelayers' truck in the tunnel. The two men were part of a gang which had completed its work for the day and was returning to base, but there was no method to check whether the tunnel was clear before the men set off. The train that hit them was pushing two trucks, so the driver had limited

The 1879 tunnel at Blaenau Ffestiniog was as expensive as it was impressive. This is the south portal amid the extensive slate waste close to the town and station. (John Alsop Collection)

visibility, compounded by the darkness of the tunnel and the smoky atmosphere. As usual, there was no hint of corporate responsibility, with most blame aimed at the supervisor of the gang for allowing his men into the tunnel; and at the decision to form the train with the engine at the rear. Abraham Evans became the fourth victim of the incident on 15 July.

The line from Betws-y-Coed is 12.5 miles long with stations at Pont-y-Pant, Dolwyddelan and Roman Bridge (now Pont Rufeinig). The Welsh spelling of Dolwyddelan did not appear on the station from 1880 after an intervention from the Willoughby family, powerful Lincolnshire-based owners of Gwydir Castle. It reverted to its proper spelling 100 years later. Apart from the tunnel, the main feature of the line is the Pont Gethin viaduct, 'a quarter of a mile long, with 32 arches, three with a 30-foot span; the Lledr river is spanned by a 90-foot arch … The viaduct has castellated piers and parapet walls, and, like the various bridges along the line, native stone enters largely into its construction,' vividly described in the *North Wales Chronicle* at the time.

The line extension formally opened with little ceremony on 22 July 1879. The GWR did not reach Blaenau Ffestiniog until October 1883. The impact on the town of three railways competing for the slate traffic caused an unflattering comment in the *London Evening Standard* in the same year. The town was 'an unsightly collection of shops and quarrymen's cottages in the midst of a huge slate quarry and has long lost all pretension to natural beauty.'

But it was slate the LNWR wanted: and it entered a shrewd arrangement to access a market with immense potential. In November 1886, the LNWR completed a slate quay at Deganwy. Euston worked with Edward Kroenke of Hamburg, a city that used Ffestiniog slate to re-roof its buildings after the 1842 fire. The LNWR opted for this quay because the German government charged one third of the duty on slate arriving by sea compared to that brought overland. It was an arrangement that justified the immense expense of the tunnel. There was a further investment in facilities in Germany with a depot on the Elbe connected to the German state railway and canal systems.

In 1870, Richard Moon, the LNWR chair, noted that 'They had woven a girdle which now completed the circle round Wales, and they had done so in a manner that would neither disturb artists or tourists. Their object had been to bring coal into North Wales and take back slates.' The line to Blaenau Ffestiniog encompassed those objectives in full. We have noted that slate was a high-volume traffic on the line, but the LNWR was fully alive to the potential of Betws-y-Coed as a tourist centre close to Snowdon, Beddgelert, Capel Curig and Porthmadog. As early as 1882, it advertised a range of circular tours completed using horse drawn carriages and the Ffestiniog Railway.

Betws-y-Coed became increasingly popular, but not without difficulty. In 1880, Jane Jarvis, aged 80, died in a fall when she got in the way of two men who were fighting each other to get on a crowded train. The line was described by the *North Wales Express* at the time as:

> One of the most romantic, and commands some of the most varied and picturesque scenery in these islands [but] there is nothing in the world more annoying to travellers than to have to run from one terminus to another, as is the case at present between the Blaenau station of the North-Western and the Diphwys station of the Festiniog and Portmadoc railways.

It was a theme that would return, as we shall see.

Richard Moon referred to the need not to disturb artists but had not anticipated the actions of John Lloyd Bond, painter one of the most popular studies of Snowdon, who disturbed the railway station in April 1883 through his drunkenness. A similar incident at a local church in 1886 finally landed him in prison with hard labour.

The scale of tourism traffic is clear from an incident, described here in the *Denbighshire Free Press* in August 1891 when:

> A heavily-loaden train from Llandudno Junction to Festiniog, crowded with excursionists … came to a standstill a little before Pontypant station on a steep incline … after several fruitless efforts the train was divided, the engine taking the first portion on to Pontypant [sic], leaving the second half standing on the dangerously steep incline below. Fortunately, the strong brakes held the second portion, crowded with scores of excursionists, till the return of the engine, and the second half was taken up to Pontypant, where the first portion had been shunted on to a siding. Here the two portions were again coupled together, and taken on to a little beyond Roman Bridge, where the gradient

Ivatt 2-6-2T 41235 approaches Blaenau Ffestiniog with a freight train in 1961. This engine was based at Llandudno Junction and withdrawn from service in November 1962. (Transport Treasury)

again reduced the speed to a snail's space, which was maintained for fully half an hour before easier gradients were reached, and the train enabled to proceed to Festiniog, where it arrived an hour late. The practice of working heavy passenger trains up the terribly steep gradients of the Festiniog line with a single engine, however economical, is fraught with danger.

Not all incidents ended so successfully. In 1881 there was a fatality close to the above incident when Benjamin Williams returned from the eisteddfod in Blaenau Ffestiniog. As his train did not stop at his home station of Roman Bridge, he decided to jump, hit his head on the last carriage and he fell dead down a steep slope near Dolwyddelan. There was more tragedy in 1900 when stationmaster Jones at Glan Conway lost his leg after he rushed to secure a loose door, tripped over a box of fish, and fell under the moving train.

Tal-y-Cafn qualified as the most dangerous spot on the line. In addition to the incidents already noted, Harriet Roberts alighted from her train at Tal-y-Cafn in 1901 distracted by news of her sister's death. The porter cleared the train to leave but did not notice she was in front of it on the level crossing with fatal consequences. The jury criticised the LNWR for not staffing the station adequately or building a bridge over the line. Unusually, the LNWR accepted responsibility and paid £100 (£10,000) in compensation. They did not build a bridge.

In July 1904, locomotive 891 with seven 6-wheeled carriages ran towards Betws-y-Coed at around 60mph to meet timetable requirements and derailed near Tal-y-Cafn. Lieutenant Colonel Yorke reported to the Board of Trade and noted that the engine left the metals and overturned, but there were only six passengers in the train, and they were in the middle of the carriages and so escaped injury. He thought that the marshy ground, a light engine, and high speed combined to cause the smash. He noted, 'Such engines cannot be regarded as express engines, and are not usually timed to run at 60mph.' He recommended that their speed be limited to 40mph.

In January 1906, Margaret Roberts and her baby died on the line near Tal-y-Cafn. Her husband had gone to buy a bottle of stout for his mother and used the railway line as a short cut. Later, he found his wife and child, killed by a train and lying on the line. Jurors sitting at the family cottage of Morfa close to the line, wondered whether there had been a domestic dispute causing Mrs Roberts to pursue her husband along the track. They concluded that witnesses had 'told the truth but not the whole truth' about this truly tragic event. Four years earlier, Richard Roberts from the same farm (and probably related) was committed to Denbigh asylum after trying to commit suicide on the adjacent railway to 'revenge his family', suggesting that this was a troubled household before the events of 1906.

A typically murky scene at Blaenau Ffestiniog North in the early 1960s as a Derby Lightweight Diesel Multiple Unit (DMU) awaits departure from the deserted station. (Transport Treasury)

On a positive note, the railway engaged in the rescue of a boating party from the river in 1910. The engine driver was approaching Tal-y-Cafn when he saw a boat in trouble on the river. He informed the stationmaster who telephoned his colleague at Glan Conwy; he sent for a local boatman who rescued all the party except Gerald Phillips, the 16-year-old son of a Bangor University professor. There were brighter moments on the line, such as in 1878 when staff discovered a crate of rotten ham and HQ ordered burial. Stationmaster Goodwin officiated as chief mourner, with other staff at Llanrwst suitably solemn as they buried the unfortunate corpses in the goods yard with due ceremony.

Of all the LNWR branches, the line to Ffestiniog was the most vulnerable to the weather. It was flooded in February 1877 between Tal-y-Cafn and Llanrwst, closed by flooding or landslip in November 1882 and notably in February 1899. 'The beautiful Vale of Conway was for miles one mass of water, while the [LNWR]

Glan Conway station in 1928 with a LNWR noticeboard despite five years under the badge of the LMS. (John Alsop Collection)

between Talycafn and Llanrwst was submerged, and traffic suspended.' As a result the LNWR 'raised the permanent way, and made it impossible for a recurrence of that interference'. Or so it thought. But in December 1905 the river washed the line away again, and it narrowly survived a flood in September 1909. Snow caused fewer problems, but the heavy fall at Llanrwst in February 1900, 'viewed through the railway carriage window … was highly picturesque [but] telegrams to and from Llandudno had to be sent by rail', suggesting that the LNWR kept its services running.

The national rail strike affected the branches to Llandudno and Blaenau Ffestiniog in August 1911, particularly because the lines depended on the Number 2 Signal Box at Llandudno Junction. Police and soldiers of the Warwickshire Regiment protected the box because 'Strikers, especially young men, had displayed

Llandudno Junction is a vital hub on the north Wales rail network and the authorities closely guarded it during the railway strike of 1911. This picture shows the busy shed at the junction in the 1930s. (John Alsop Collection)

a threatening attitude, and were believed to be contemplating putting No 2 cabin out of action, which would have blocked the Llandudno and Ffestiniog branches.'

The larger conflict of the 1914-18 war saw most input from the railways along the coast, where there were significant encampments. The most important support for the war effort along the Conwy valley was at Dolgarrog, where a station opened in December 1916 to connect with a short line across the river to an aluminium smelting plant in the village. The works were supplied by water from a reservoir on the adjacent hillside which burst and flooded the village causing sixteen deaths in 1925.

It is surprising that the thriving slate town of Bethesda was not among the first places to benefit from a standard gauge branch line from the CHR. During the

Dolgarrog station opened in 1916 to allow access to the aluminium works that was vital for the war effort. A short line extended west of the station and crossed the river. **(WRRC)**

1850s there seemed little public demand, but by 1860 frustration had begun to surface, as reported here in the *North Wales Chronicle*:

> Probably, there is no place in the Principality that has improved more than Bethesda during the last five or six years; hundreds of excellent houses have been erected; several of which would serve as model cottages. [Bethesda] has its Local Board of Commissioners, who carefully enquire into the draining and general improvement of the town and neighbourhood: gas also has been introduced. The whole place appears in a prosperous and flourishing condition, but the greatest drawback at present is the want of a railway branch line from the [CHR].

In the same issue, another correspondent noted that there was not even a station at Llandygai, the nearest point to Bethesda on the main line – apparently because of opposition from slate-owner Lord Penrhyn – and called for a public meeting to start a campaign. But the silence continued, and it took until 1865 to start a regular omnibus service. 'Carrying 25 passengers … four times each way, daily, meeting, and returning from the most important trains. Bethesda has become a great place of business, and … It is a great wonder to us that some spirited individual has not started one long before.'

Nonetheless, it was 1876 before there was a concerted effort to create a railway and to understand the reason for the delay. There was a large meeting in the Magistrates' Rooms in Bangor with many local worthies present and one notable absentee, Lord Penrhyn, who owned the quarries at Bethesda. The meeting was in favour of the railway and explored options for it.

Two obstacles exposed key stresses at the heart of society in north Wales at this time. The first was the difficulty of developing any railway without the support of the LNWR, the largest industrial corporation in the world, and a model of nineteenth-century enterprise that focused on the needs of metropolis. The second was the need to secure the backing of the Pennant family, headed by Lord Penrhyn of Penrhyn Castle. The Pennants owned the land and quarries between Bangor and Bethesda and stood for a much older form of power; paternalistic landlordism with echoes of suffocating feudalism that demanded – and often got – deference from local people. Penrhyn sacked eighty quarrymen who voted Liberal against his wishes in 1868. Like others we have noted, the Pennants derived a substantial part of their wealth from sugar plantations in Jamaica and received £15,000 (£1.6million) compensation in 1838 for loss of slaves.

Neither of these great powers attended the April 1876 meeting where the pressure came from an emerging third force of smaller middle class business owners who resented the power of big business and landownership, 'the commercial and trading interests of Bangor' as one participant put it. William Cadwaladr Davies, who had links to the *North Wales Chronicle* and the later formation of the university in Bangor, convened the meeting. The local leaders of working people such as William Parry, who helped to form the North Wales Quarrymen's Union in 1876, supported the movement for a Bethesda railway. Parry noted that locals had proposed a railway for some time but 'for some reason or other it had been deferred'. His colleague, workers' leader Morgan Richards, made clear his support for a standard gauge line and wanted to expose the obstacle to it:

Why was there not a line already? He ventured to say there were no such place in the kingdom as Bethesda and Bangor are without being connected by railway. Was there something in the nature of the ground to prevent the construction of a railway? No, then there must be some other cause, and he thought the meeting ought to be put in possession of that cause.

He then explained his own understanding of the problem. 'They knew the land belonged to one owner, and that he declined to sell it, but they also knew that it was possible to obtain an Act of Parliament which would give them power to acquire land to construct a railway.' So Penrhyn's opposition was the main problem and had been so from the beginning, but only in 1876 when more people had the vote and labour was more organised could that reason become public.

The meeting also heard that Penrhyn would agree to a railway, but only a narrow-gauge one. No doubt he knew that only the LNWR could supply a competing line and that it would only do so on the standard gauge. It was simply a blocking tactic to agree to a narrow-gauge line. The meeting agreed that the LNWR should build the line and that Penrhyn had to support it. They deployed one ingenious tactic to influence him, a suggestion that a line could be made from Bethesda to Caernarfon, the centre of his great rival slate owner Assheton-Smith of Vaynol. There was another meeting soon after the first one at which Penrhyn consented to a line but hedged it with conditions that affected its viability: no free or cheap land; no slates transported on it; no station anywhere near Penrhyn Castle; and no connection with Port Penrhyn.

It became clear to a later meeting that the LNWR had already insisted in January 1876 that 'the restrictions imposed by Lord Penrhyn are such as to prevent the company from entertaining your proposal to construct the suggested line of railway'. The battle lines between industrial and feudal power were clear in a further reply in which the LNWR stated, 'It [the line] will have to be constructed in such manner as this Company may deem most advisable and must be free from all obligations as to the position of the stations, etc.'

The committee then raised the spectre of a line to Caernarfon by noting that a prospectus had been issued headed, 'Railway Communication from Bethesda via Pentir, Rhiwlas, Bethel, and Llanddeiniolen, to Carnarvon'. It also applied pressure to the LNWR via a suggestion that the GWR might build a line from Corwen to Bangor via Betws-y-Coed and Bethesda. Unmoved, the LNWR intimated that the price asked for the land by Penrhyn was too high. His lordship added further complexity by beginning to construct a narrow-gauge freight-only line, causing the local paper to suggest that Lord Penrhyn should simply upgrade it. Again, no action followed.

The standard-gauge project did not re-emerge until November 1878 as the economy was sinking and Penrhyn's objections had caused Bethesda residents to favour a link to Caernarfon. Once again the scheme stalled and in December 1878 the GWR declined to be involved. At the same time, there was a meeting at Penrhyn Castle at which the elements of the dispute were clear and Penrhyn's position appeared more reasonable. He pointed out that his estate was legally obliged to charge a fair price for the land and made interesting and valid points about the LNWR's ambition to monopolise the carriage of slate, and the impact that would have on coastal shipping in north Wales. He shared his conversation with Richard Moon, the LNWR chair with the *North Wales Chronicle*:

> [Penrhyn] "No, I shall certainly not give up the carriage of my slates." Mr Moon said, "Why not?" I said, "I will tell you why, Mr Moon. My reason is that I like to manage my own affairs instead of having them managed for me at Euston Square." If I had done as the Company wished me to do what would have been the state of things at Bangor? The port would have been quite cut out. The Company would not have given any great facilities to the port or shipping of Bangor. Indeed, if all the slates were carried by the [LNWR] at whatever terms they liked to enforce, the whole of the shipping interest here would have been cut off.

Faced with this impasse, the people of Bethesda increasingly favoured a direct rail link with Caernarfon in January 1879. Meanwhile, Penrhyn proceeded with an upgraded narrow-gauge line with steam traction to Hirael to serve his port at Bangor, thus reducing the possibility of the LNWR capturing the slate traffic from Bethesda.

A year later, Penrhyn made a further move to undermine the drive for a standard gauge railway to either Caernarfon or Bangor. Though he had previously said that his new line would be unsuitable for passengers, he granted access to the Quarrymen's Car Society to run its own workmen's trains on the line between Bangor and Bethesda. The nature of the relationship between Penrhyn and his workers was clear in the latter's loyal address in which they extolled 'Lord Penrhyn's generosity and kindness [that] flew down to them as a society [and] exhorted the members to refrain from committing any unworthy act that would tend to occasion the withdrawal of the advantages they now enjoyed.' Those advantages did not include carriages with protection from the weather or suspension to make the ride easier.

Penrhyn's earlier reservations about the suitability of the line for passengers proved correct when David Griffiths died in a collision that injured seven others near Bethesda in August 1888. As usual, human error was the conclusion of the inquest.

Despite these obstructions, by July 1880, Richard Moon was walking the line between Bangor and Bethesda with a view to work starting on the new LNWR line as

Feudal power meets industrial strength – Lord Penrhyn's narrow-gauge railway and the LNWR's Cegin viaduct seen in 1953. The LNWR Bethesda branch joined the CHR close to the viaduct. **(LNWR Society)**

soon as possible. A year later, the LNWR had awarded the contract to Messrs Nelson and Co of Carlisle at a cost of £70,000 (£6.9million) and starting around 100 yards east of Bangor tunnel near Llandygai. Unsurprisingly, Euston ignored all local tenders. The line was five miles long with a tunnel and viaduct near Coetmor Bridge, where the line crossed the Ogwen river. There were stations at Felin Hen and Tregarth.

This troublesome line presented further challenges before completion. The Tregarth part of the line was 'the scene of very extensive and successful blasting operations [in September 1881]. The line at this place is most vigorously proceeded with, a great number of men being employed … Noble's [Nobel's] Blasting Gelatine [was evaluated] and the result convinced all present that the gelatine's disruptive force is really enormous.'

Robert Griffiths of Tregarth realised this all too well in 1881 when he died from a rock fall after a blast in the cutting at Felin Hen. Isaac Jones of Cardiganshire died in the Coetmor Tunnel in a dynamite explosion, a common cause of death in such operations. 15-year-old local resident Thomas Hughes died a month later at the same site after wagons ran over him.

There was a hint of obstruction from Penrhyn in a court case in which he sued the contractors for taking too long to unload stone shipped from Annan. There was only one crane available at the port and Penrhyn's staff were using it constantly, so contractors brought another crane from Conwy. The contractors were able to show the court they acted reasonably. In January 1884, a ballast engine was pushing two trucks up the incline to Tregarth and was derailed, seriously injuring the stoker and a man named Roberts. In the same month, poachers (reckoned to be construction workers) stole a large quantity of dynamite from the tunnel works for use in the local river to kill salmon. As the line neared completion in 1884, the most serious incident occurred when a part of Coetmor tunnel collapsed after heavy rain, killing Richard Evans of Amlwch and injuring four of his colleagues. David Griffiths found the 1880 Employers Liability Act useful when he sued the contractors for injuries received on the Bethesda line. The jury awarded him £140 (£13,250). By August 1883 the whole of the excavation had been removed, 15 of the 22 bridges were built, and the Bethesda tunnel was lined for one half the length of 298 yards. The *Carnarvon and Denbigh Herald* reported that misfortune even blighted the opening:

> A rather serious accident occurred through the giving way of a valve on the contractor's engine. One of the men who was on the engine was badly scalded, and Mr Wood, brother to the contractor's representative, in jumping down caught his foot, and had a nasty fall on the ballast, his head being injured.

Once opened, the line ran with few problems. Quarryman William Hughes was returning from the Congregational Festival at Caernarfon in 1885 and stepped onto the viaduct parapet near Felin Hen believing he was at the station when the train stopped. He fell into the river below and narrowly escaped death. But for the event he had attended, one might have suspected drink as a factor in such a bizarre accident. Tragically, Ann Davies of Tregarth died by her own hand in the tunnel at Coetmor in July 1900.

The railway supplied the means for both the authorities and the strikers to mobilise during the longest industrial strike in British history at Penrhyn's quarries between 1900 and 1903. In August 1901, 500 troops arrived in Bethesda by train, as did Labour leader Keir Hardie and his daughter to support the strikers. Tregarth station was the scene of a serious affray related to the strike in January 1902 when quarry workers met a group of men, women and children leaving the Bangor train, which was reported in the *Manchester Evening News*:

> A huge fight ... ensued, in the course of which several combatants and women were hurled on to the line between the carriages, one woman sustaining a severe cut on the head. Kicks and blows were freely distributed, and the police were helpless ... officers of Hussars [from Bangor] went to Bethesda to take command of the detachment permanently stationed there.

It was to no avail, as Bethesda station was at the centre of a fight between strikers, police, and soldiers in September. In an interesting sequel, a train from Bethesda stopped near Felin Hen in 1904 after a serious fight between two men from different sides of the great strike – one had worked, and one had struck. The struggle between them proved difficult to contain and was not helped by the fact

Bethesda station is quiet in this picture as the end of passenger services approached, in contrast to its riotous involvement in the bitter strike of 1902. Coal engine 58903 started as LNWR 966 at Crewe in 1885 and ended its service in June 1954. (Online Transport Archive)

Felin Hen station in the latter days of the LNWR. It was not so peaceful in 1904 when a train stopped after a serious fight between two men from opposite sides in the great slate strike. (John Alsop Collection)

that the train stopped on an incline and could not restart, delaying its arrival in Bangor by over an hour. A couple of months later, the state of impoverishment in the area was indicated by Joseph Roberts aged 15 who was a 'learner' on no money at Tregarth, apparently a common practice on the LNWR at this time. He succumbed to the temptation of handling money and stole 4s but as he was of good character the court discharged him without punishment.

From the end of the quarry dispute to the demise of the LNWR in 1923 there was little of note to report on the Bethesda branch. It had been a long struggle to secure this short railway and the needs of local people and small businesses seemed to be secondary to the power struggle between the great feudal landowner

There was mayhem at Tregarth Station during the industrial action in 1902 but the station is empty and closed fifty years later. In 2023 it was the site of a community centre. (Online Transport Archive)

at Penrhyn Castle and the industrial power of Euston Square. Without that tension, there would have been a railway to Bethesda long before 1884. After it survived the quarry strike and the First World War, the line faced a challenge that would be more difficult to overcome and noted by the *Western Mail* in May 1922. 'The railway fare from Bangor to Bethesda is ninepence; by motorbus it is only sixpence.' By then, the powers of both Penrhyn and Euston were fading.

Chapter 5

The Western Slate District and Anglesey

'The last link in the iron ring that now weds Wales to England'
Carnarvon and Denbigh Herald 9 July 1870

'Not until the Saxons of old got hold of [Anglesey] were they ever able to hold and to keep possession of the country and this *railway* now penetrated through its very heart.'
North Wales Chronicle 17 December 1864

The area south of Bangor was rich in potential slate traffic and one where transport innovation had already shown the value of experimenting with diverse ways to carry this cumbersome cargo. Those developments, such as the Dinorwic Railway (1824), Nantlle Railway (NR) (1829), and the Festiniog Railway (FR) (1832) had aimed at more efficient ways to get the slate to convenient seaports at Porth Dinorwic, Caernarfon and Porthmadog, respectively. The aim of the LNWR was different. As we have seen, it created a large slate distribution centre at Mold Junction on the CHR in 1852 and a quay at Deganwy specifically aimed at the lucrative German market in 1886. Both those developments challenged the existing quasi-feudal power structure of the slate industry in north Wales and the thriving coastal sea traffic. In this chapter we shall see how the competition to transport slate changed because of the arrival of the LNWR on the Lleyn Peninsula. As with the area between Mold and Llandudno Junction, we shall also encounter the LNWR's concern that a rival railway network might emerge in north Wales to challenge its monopoly. This chapter will extend to examining the growth of the LNWR in Anglesey, which does not fit into the pattern of other branch developments from the main line between Chester and Holyhead as the BTB protected the company from rival projects on the island.

At the end of the first chapter, we saw that the CHR had toyed with the NWR, a scheme to build a line from Bangor to Caernarfon and on to Porth Dinllaen if the BTB failed. We now examine how that scheme, at least as far as Caernarfon,

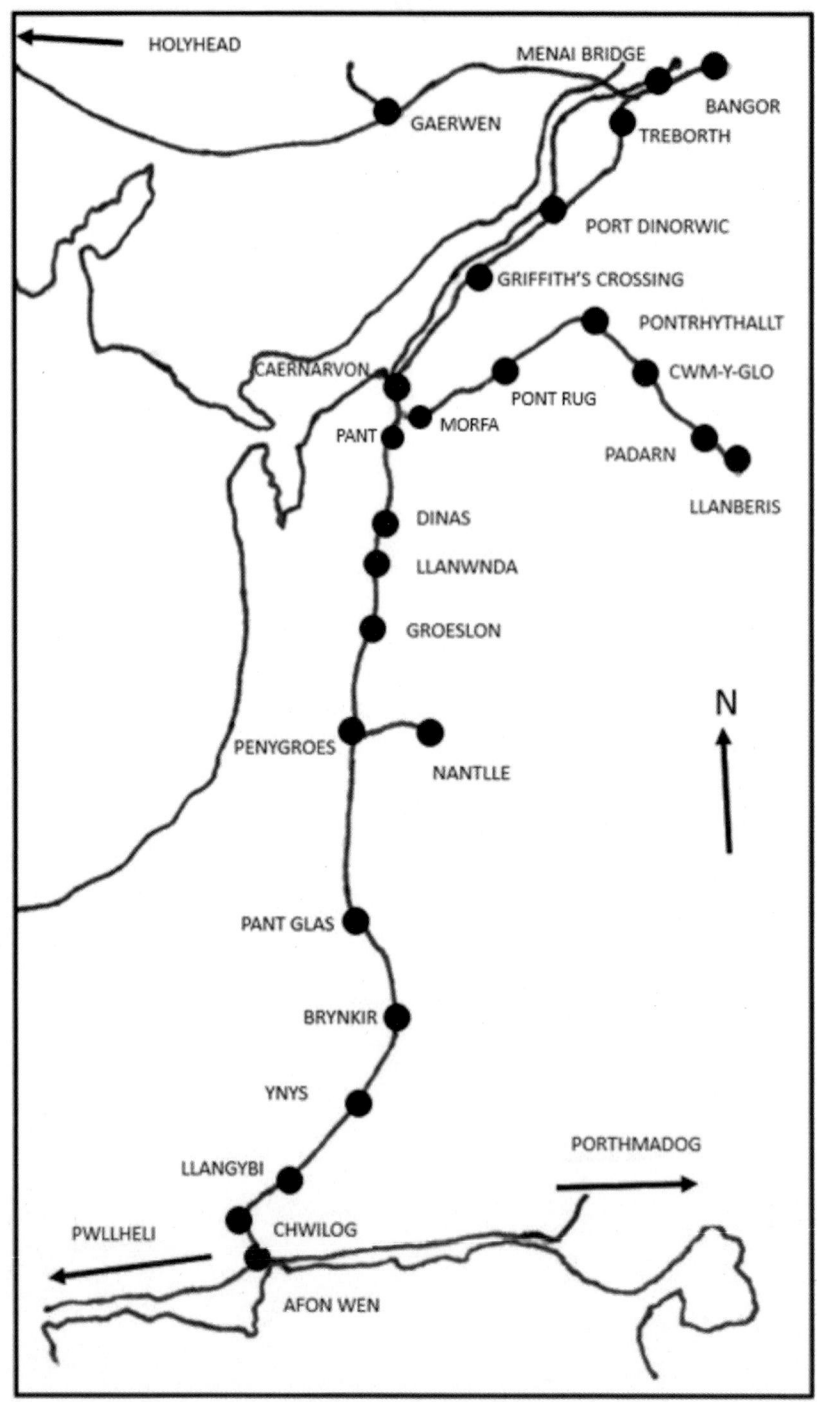

Map 4: The Western Slate District: showing LNWR stations c1910.

revived after the corruption and double-dealing of the NWR had brought its initial downfall.

The BTB opened in March 1850 and within six months plans for a line from Bangor to Caernarfon were before parliament. The *North Wales Chronicle* hoped it was a scheme 'so often projected, and as often abandoned, [that] will now ... be carried out'. The prospects for completion improved because of the 'full sanction and concurrence of the directors of the [CHR] for their undertaking, although [the Carnarvon Railway] transactions are perfectly independent of the latter' – a dubious claim. The line was to leave the CHR near the BTB, through Treborth with a tunnel at Capel-y-Graig, close to the Vaynol Lodge gate and:

> Passing the inclined plane of [slate quarry owner] Mr [Assheton] Smith's railway at Port Dinorwic, [who] has most handsomely come forward, and munificently offered free of cost, the whole of that portion of his land which the line would traverse and also in every way [helped] to forward and promote the formation of the line'.

The line from Bangor to Caernarfon had few construction difficulties beyond the Vaynol Tunnel and some impressive architecture, as seen here at Pandy Lane crossing in the 1970s. Staff are clearing the way for a freight train headed by Class 24 D5146 which went out of service in 1976. **(Transport Treasury)**

Port Dinorwic new station – an impressive replacement for the smaller structure in 1873 – and closed in 1960, ahead of many other stations on the line. **(John Alsop Collection)**

Here was the major reason for its success for, as we have seen, the later line to Bethesda failed initially because Lord Penrhyn refused to give land for the line or support its construction except on the strictest terms. Thus, by January 1851 the *Carnarvon and Denbigh Herald* report showed the necessity of landowner support:

> The arrangements for carrying out this undertaking are at last completed and … the whole of the deposit required by [Assheton-Smith] … has been placed in the Carnarvon Old Bank; and the contract for making this portion of the line has been signed by the contracting parties—to be completed by the end of 1851.

When it received a second reading in parliament in February, it became the Bangor and Carnarvon Railway (BCR). By March, the CHR meeting heard that it expected 100,000 tons of slate traffic annually.

The start of construction was troublesome. In May 1851, English and Welsh labourers struck because of the employment of Irish navvies, coinciding with a more violent disturbance for similar reasons at Holyhead on the breakwater works. The cause was apparently not financial but was rather the 'natural antipathy [against] the sons of Erin [but nonetheless] the line is proceeding satisfactorily, particularly the tunnel near the Vaynol Lodge'. The contractors missed the hoped-for Christmas completion in 1851 but by March 1852 a train ran between Bangor and Port Dinorwic.

This section opened in April 1852 and the impact on the locals was especially noteworthy, as was the patronising tone of the report in the *North Wales Chronicle*:

> The noise of the shrill whistle and panting of the iron horse being heard for the first time in this district, much interest was excited amongst the peasantry, crowds of whom assembled on the banks and bridges which commanded a view of the approaching monster. A puff of steam being thrown off at Dinorwic … caused a momentary alarm, followed by peals of laughter.

There were greater festivities when the line opened to Caernarfon in July, with remarkably few accidents and incidents during its construction. The CHR arranged terms favourable to the owners of the BCR but by September 1853 wished to lease the line directly for £6,000 per year (£631,000) rather than grant traffic receipts.

And passenger numbers must also have been positive as stations opened at Treborth and Griffith's Crossing in February 1854. Given the power of the landed gentry in the district, it is probable that the company built these stations for their convenience. There were three big estates locally – Treborth estate and Llanfair Hall both close to the new stations and Glynllifon, the home of Lord Newborough, near Llanwnda station. It was here that Princess Victoria arrived in 1888 on a private visit, accompanied by LNWR's District Superintendent Dent. The landowners showed their power when the LNWR attempted to close Treborth station in 1858 on the opening of the nearby station at Menai Bridge. Owner Mary Crawley defeated the railway in court. A similar fate befell the mighty LNWR, which absorbed the BCR in 1867 when it refused to carry building materials to the station for a later owner in 1901.

Sadly, the good safety record of the line did not survive its completion. In May 1853, platelayer Hugh Daniel died under the 9.30am train from Bangor near the level crossing at Llanfair Hall. He was with a gang of labourers but did not move from the track when the engine whistle sounded. Bangor stationmaster Oldham told the coroner that the contractors would defray the funeral expenses of the deceased, and colleagues would make a collection for Mr Daniel's widow.

Treborth station deserves special mention for its longevity, surviving at least three attempts to close it from 1858. BR finally saw it off in 1959, around the time of this picture. **(LNWR Society)**

William Anwyl, stationmaster at Griffith's Crossing, met a similar fate in May 1859. His station was a request stop from June 1854 and as the 6pm train approached there were no passengers, so Mrs Anwyl arranged the informal signal to the driver not to stop. As the train approached, she saw her husband rush across the line in front of the train trying to save Catherine Evans, an elderly woman who had entered the station gate and begun to cross the line. Both died instantly. The coroner found that William Anwyl should have locked the gate and so he bore responsibility for the accident. He also noted that the signal used at the station was not authorised by the company and should cease. Stoker David Jones fell off his engine at the same place in November 1865 and died two weeks later after amputation of his arm. In 1871, the LNWR decided to double the BCR, and two men died in the construction of the second bore of the Vaynol Tunnel, each by jumping from a spoil heap onto a moving train in the summer of 1872.

Above and below: *Llanwnda saw royalty in 1888 when Princess Victoria visited Lord Newborough. Those glories have faded in these pictures from the early sixties (north towards the bridge). The station signs are from the LMS era.* **(WRRC)**

Staff take elaborate care at Griffith's Crossing in 1969 as D1693 prepares to cross with a freight train. Less so in 1854 when stationmaster Anwyl died while trying to save an elderly passenger crossing in front of a train. **(Transport Treasury)**

Vaynol Tunnel was the main challenge to engineers between Bangor and Caernarfon. The LNWR added a second bore in 1872 that cost the lives of two men. **(LNWR Society)**

The LNWR alleged Port Dinorwic was a station where people tended to leave moving trains. In December 1869 John Jones had jumped to avoid paying his fare, just a week after another man had lost a leg doing something similar. In 1886, Mrs Jones from Brynrodyn post office, and wife of the local vicar, died under a fish truck at Groeslon Station, but as usual there was a simple inquest and a routine 'accidental death' verdict.

Griffiths' Crossing station was also the site of the last moments of a young bull that had strayed onto the line. The event caused the *North Wales Chronicle* to recall in October 1865 an anecdote from engineer George Stephenson before a House of Commons Committee during the proceedings for an early railway:

> Old George said that he was certain [trains] would travel at the rate of at least 12 miles an hour, and ... could be made to travel at even thirty miles an hour. This assertion was [regarded] as the wild dream of a theorizing enthusiast; [causing one MP to ask him] would it not be a bad thing if, when going at that great speed the engine should chance to run against a cow on the line, "Yes sir", the old man rejoined, "it would be a very bad thing for the coo (sic)".

Groeslon station where Mrs Jones from the local Post Office died under a fish truck in 1886. Passengers and staff feature in this posed picture from the LNWR's heyday. (John Alsop Collection)

There were slate quarries close to Caernarfon that could benefit from access to the standard gauge railway network, and it was not long before the pressure mounted to take the line south towards Pwllheli or south-east to Porthmadog. To the south, the quarries of Nantlle benefited from the NR, opened in 1828 – even before the more famous FR – and carrying enormous quantities of slate in horse drawn wagons to the quay at Caernarfon. The lack of steam traction caused increasing frustration that generated pressure for a main line towards the expected railway along the Cambrian coast to Pwllheli.

Influential quarry and landowners met in Pwllheli in March 1858 and supported a proposal for a railway from Porthmadog to Caernarfon via that town. There were offers of free land from many and support from the owners of the NR for some of that route becoming part of the new line, named as the Carnarvonshire Railway, (CR) with Charles Spooner (of the FR) as engineer. The meeting of the company in September 1860 placed it on a collision course with the LNWR. Curiously, the meeting was addressed by George Hammond Whalley who we saw in Chapter 2 acting *for* the LNWR in presenting a spoiler line between Ruabon and Llangollen in 1859. In this meeting, Whalley supported the creation of the amalgamation of Welsh railways that the LNWR and GWR would work hard to destroy during the 1860s. As Whalley told the meeting, reported here by the *Eddowes Shrewsbury Journal*:

> The proposed Welsh Coast Railway was intended to connect Porth Dinllaen and the intervening district down to Aberystwyth with the railways in course of construction, or which were in contemplation to that town from Milford Haven on the south and with the midland district, such Hereford, Worcester, Oxford, and the various lines of which these places were the central points … He could scarcely believe that [blocking up the] great outlet of this district, would have the sanction or support of the [LNWR]. He had … faith in the liberal and enlightened views of that great company.

Bearing in mind the approach we saw adopted by the LNWR to any scheme that threatened its monopoly elsewhere in north Wales, it is difficult to see how Whalley could have genuinely had such faith.

This was a period of feverish railway activity in north Wales, and the western slate districts were fully engaged in the process. The schemes were summarised in the *North Wales Chronicle* as a 'Christmas Pie' in January 1861 with uncertainty as to which were the 'plums'. It considered Welsh railways were at a crossroads and the main problem was the dominance of the LNWR in the north and the GWR in the south. The solution proposed was the 'third force' because:

The country is in want of a line of railway, to be continued on from Carnarvon to the south coast of Carnarvonshire; that it be extended on each side respectively, to Porthdinllaen to Portmadoc, that from Portmadoc be taken down the coast to Barmouth, Towyn, Aberystwyth and Milford Haven and that branch lines be constructed from this main trunk line to Machynlleth, in order to connect with the Montgomeryshire system, and also another to Dolgelley, Bala, and Corwen there to join the Denbigh and Corwen line on the one side, and the Corwen and Llangollen branch on the other.

That, of course, was precisely the scheme that Euston and Paddington were determined to thwart. There seemed some evidence that the LNWR exerted influence through a strong connection with the NR, with the *North Wales Chronicle* suggesting that it had leased the line. Whether it had done so is not clear but there seemed a possible connection with the CHR and LNWR whose solicitor Richard Preston represented the NR in court when appealing against it paying local rates and referred to Edward Preston as the lessee of the company. Their having similar surnames was not coincidental – Richard Preston had an older brother called Edward – and the tactic of inserting a supportive figure on a smaller railway board was an LNWR practice, as we have seen.

When the Pwllheli meeting reconvened in January 1861 there were moves to promote a line from Pwllheli to Penygroes by associates of the NR who were in league with the LNWR. The concern in Pwllheli was that the LNWR and NR would prevent a through line from Caernarfon to Pwllheli and when the chair commented that the best line was 'one which would be free of the [LNWR]', he received loud cheers for this and further allegations of Euston's guiding hand at the NR. In the same edition of the paper there was reference to a meeting at which attendees asked Mr Richardson, representing the NR, to give an assurance that traffic from the south could use his proposed line. He could not do so, even on the offer of being engineer for the whole scheme. There was evidence here of the LNWR trying to prevent a through line from Pwllheli to Caernarfon, while nominally staying out of the conflict.

Nonetheless, the LNWR faced a stiff contest once Benjamin Piercy obtained investment and parliamentary attention by April 1861 for his line on the Cambrian coast with an extension to Porth Dinllaen but not, at that stage, Caernarfon, because of opposition from the NR and the Admiralty, with the latter not agreeing to a line across the harbour. Another meeting in Pwllheli heard that the Admiralty opposition could be overcome by approaching Caernarfon from Penygroes rather than Porth Dinllaen. By November 1861 both the CR, broadly representing the interests of the Welsh Coast group, and the NR, backed by the LNWR, were advertising schemes to connect Porthmadog, Pwllheli and Caernarfon. Piercy summed up the situation at a meeting in Pwllheli in March 1862 when he stated his view that his intention was to open up the country whereas the NR was intent on preventing railway development because the competition would reduce its profit.

Disingenuously, Piercy praised the LNWR, which was surely supportive of the NR stance. Nonetheless, Piercy thought, as this *North Wales Chronicle* piece shows, that:

> Many of the [LNWR] Directors ... and several of the officials were capable, to his own personal knowledge, of taking an advanced and enlightened view of railway management; and he believed that liberal and wise counsels would ultimately prevail in that Company in reference to the railway system in [north Wales]. He felt sure that a larger trade could be brought to Porthdinllaen than Holyhead now commands, and ... if the [LNWR] secured communication between Carnarvon and Porthdinllaen, they would get a traffic which would fully compensate them for any loss through Holyhead.

Piercy was trying to weaken the alliance between the NR and LNWR and understood the LNWR would never back a rival harbour to Holyhead at Porth Dinllaen.

The *North Wales Chronicle* regarded Piercy's contribution as 'a remarkable one throughout, being candid and straightforward to a degree, with not the least tincture of professional mystery or circumlocution about it' and it seemed sympathetic to Piercy's charge against the NR of it trying to 'block up' Caernarfon, Pwllheli and Porthmadog, strikingly similar to the charge of 'blocking up the vale' [of Clwyd] made against the LNWR noted in chapter 2. One such charge might be circumstantial, two or more looks like a Euston policy. Piercy's position did seem reasonable: to extend the railway from Porthmadog to Porth Dinllaen; leave the link between Pwllheli and Caernarfon to the NR scheme; and then agree running rights over each other's lines.

Conflict continued between the NR and the Welsh Coast group, but the latter gained the upper hand when its legislation passed in July 1862. The *North Wales Chronicle* was exuberant:

> The Welsh Coast system will not only connect North and South Wales and open an outlet from the Coast and mid parts of the country into England, but it will accommodate an extended range of the country ... it girdles the whole coast up to Portmadoc, and from thence on to Pwllheli and Porthdinllaen,

which is its great western terminus, and where a large and commodious harbour is to be made. From near the ancient town of Criccieth a fork line, of primary importance, will be constructed to Carnarvon where it will join the [LNWR] by which junction there will be an unbroken route from all parts of the coast of Wales and the contiguous districts on its course to Chester and all parts of the Kingdom.

Above and below: *Penygroes station in LNWR days, where the line to Afon Wen started in 1864. There is a substantial staff group on this small station in the view north. The fuller view south shows the Nantlle branch to the left and the extensive sidings to the right.* (John Alsop Collection)

Legislation was one thing and construction quite another. The priorities of Piercy and engineer Thomas Savin were along the Cambrian coast so that the link with Pwllheli and Porthmadog did not start until December 1864 at Penygroes.

Thomas Jones of the NR was present showing its consent to the incorporation of its own line into the new route. In February 1865, contractors made progress between Penygroes and Pant Glas, and between Chwilog and Afon Wen employing several hundred men. By July 1865, Pwllheli saw its first navvies and anticipated 'the shrill whistle of the train [as] the herald of a kind of millennial era to dawn upon us'. But one of the main components of the scheme – the harbour at Porth Dinllaen – was struggling to gain national recognition and the funding that such status might attract, no doubt affected by the power of the Holyhead lobby and the immense government funding for the breakwater there that was still eight years from completion.

By March 1866, a *North Wales Chronicle* reporter secured a trip on the nearly completed line from Bontnewydd (the northern terminus at that time), noting plans for stations at Pwllheli Road (in 1877 it became Llanwnda), Groeslon, Penygroes (as spelt from 1904), Bryncir and extensions to Nefyn and Abersoch (never built). At that stage there was no plan for a station at the junction with the Cambrian coast railway. This account omitted any reference to Porth Dinllaen. There was special mention of the engine constructed at the Atlas works in Manchester and named *Castell Deudraeth* after the home of the company chair. The account considered that the line was close to completion but thought opening by June 1866 was optimistic bearing in mind the need for formal inspection.

The author of that account could hardly have expected events to endorse his words about inspection so dramatically in September 1866. The Calvinistic Methodist Association held its quarterly meeting in Caernarfon over three days and attracted vast crowds, including over 700 who travelled by train from the Porthmadog area. They had pressed contractor Thomas Savin to run a train over the uninspected route. He agreed and organised the excursion himself with his brother John on the footplate. The train consisted of eighteen open ballast wagons, with planks across them for seats. *Castell Deudraeth* hauled the train which reached Pant station – the nearest open station to Caernarfon – without difficulty. On its return trip in foul weather, the train stopped to take water just beyond Bryncir station and left the track after crossing faulty points. Despite the low speed, a derailment caused injuries to many, and six deaths, the second worst rail accident in north Wales after the Abergele crash of August 1868.

The immense sympathy felt for the Savins and their efforts to bring railways to Wales played a part in Thomas escaping blame for running a heavily loaded train on an unapproved line. The coroner summed up the evidence at the inquest in a manner that left little room for Savin to escape, but the jury preferred to believe that the deliberate placing of a stone in the mechanism caused the accident. The Board of Trade inspector rejected that suggestion and concluded that the failure of an employee to reset the points for the return journey caused the derailment. The inspector also found that the company used the uninspected railway between Caernarfon, Pwllheli and Porthmadog several times for the armed forces and the local gentry, and it was on one of these earlier excursions that Savin agreed to supply transport for the Calvinist conference.

At this time, Thomas Savin also faced the Overend Gurney bank collapse and the CR had to seek extra time to complete its work. The chaos in Welsh railways during this period was extreme but by autumn 1866 the CR, NR and Cambrian Railways wanted formal amalgamation. Inspectors found the CR line incomplete, as it was also in December 1866. It was not until 2 September 1867 that the line opened, but the poor service muted any celebration, as this report in the *North Wales Chronicle* shows:

> Great complaints are continually being made as to the irregularity of the trains, upon the 'time' on which not the slight dependence can be placed. From all accounts it is not reduced to a question of minutes as on other lines, but it is often a question of hours. Not only do the trains run slowly, [and]

The greatest hazard at deserted Brynkir station in this picture is extreme cold, hence the fire devil next to the water tank in the 1960s. In 1866, six passengers died here after a crowded train left the tracks. (LNWR Society)

there is much irregularity in starting ... As regards the line being opened to 'Carnarvon' that at present is not strictly the fact. The trains start from the Pant Station, which is fully a mile and a half from the Carnarvon Railway Station, and this causes an immense amount of inconvenience. ... The Company has completed the line to the Morfa, near the town, and they have built a bridge over the river Seiont, but there is no station at the terminus ... It is now rumoured in the town that an understanding has been come to with the [LNWR, who] are disposed to make a tunnel under the town for the use of both the Llanberis line and the Carnarvonshire one. [This] will take a long time to make, and probably it and the Llanberis line will be finished at one and the same time ... It is some consolation to know that Mr Moreton, Sportsman Hotel, runs an omnibus from the Station in Carnarvon to the Pant Station, to meet the trains advertised to arrive.

This comment points to two further developments that completed the standard gauge network in this area and the LNWR's domination of it. The first is the interest of the LNWR in the CR and the way that it ensured that it did not benefit at once from access to the centre of Caernarfon, which would have added to the value of the line from Pwllheli. At least one correspondent to the *North Wales Chronicle* thought it was not accidental that the LNWR Caernarfon to Bangor train left just before passengers alighting at the Pant station could make the connection by bus and such mean-spiritedness would have been consistent with the LNWR tactics in railway competition.

The race to meet the train had fatal consequences for Robert Jones, one of the bus drivers. He died after the bus went out of control. 'The road between the stations, with at least one frightful hill [that] was never intended for four or five omnibuses to travel continually, at full speed (generally necessary, in order to catch the next train).' CR engine driver McCafferty and the train guard Godfrey (sitting next to Jones) were lucky to survive.

Second, by the time of this incident LNWR pressure had produced a Wharncliffe Meeting – a company meeting under parliamentary standing orders to approve a bill conferring new powers – which gave Euston greater access to the CR. By August 1868, the Carnarvon and Llanberis Railway (CLR) had arrangements with the LNWR for a line to connect at Caernarfon with the CLR and the CR and to strengthen the Tan-y-bryn bridge, near Penygroes. By March 1869, the CR meeting voted James Bancroft, a director of the LNWR, onto the CR board; a man whose appointment on the board of a Welsh railway usually presaged a takeover by Euston. Richard Dean, an LNWR director, joined at the same meeting.

In 1867 the line from Afon Wen stopped frustratingly short of Caernarfon at Pant – this is the site in the 1950s with an original building. (LNWR Society)

By November 1869, the LNWR had sought powers to take over the CR and the CLR, drop the NR and create its own short branch to Nantlle. The LNWR made the motive clear at its meeting in February 1869. 'An opportunity of obtaining an interest in the [CR] having presented itself, the directors have deemed it advisable to avail themselves of it. Access to the large slate traffic of the Nantlle Valley, hitherto carried almost exclusively by water, will thus be secured to the company.' It was a stretch to say the opportunity had 'presented itself', given the LNWR's persistent machinations.

The CR held its meetings at Euston until the inevitable takeover occurred in August 1870. The formal opening of the connecting line in Caernarfon just preceded this transaction, celebrated in the town in July 1870. Only one ship in the harbour displayed bunting, a sign of the damage the local shipowners expected to their share of slate traffic. By contrast, the LNWR hierarchy was out in force to celebrate 'the last link in the iron ring that now weds Wales to England [and the] possibility of trains, previously stopped by [an] awkward break at Carnarvon, making the complete tour of Wales'. There was no acknowledgement that the LNWR caused this 'awkward break' of course. The LNWR demonstrated its priority by holding the meeting in Llanberis from where it expected the bulk of its revenue to come, rather than Caernarfon where three railways – the BCR, the CR and the CLR – met.

A railway connection to Llanberis was an obvious project in the 1860s because of the enormous quantities of slate quarried there and the need for main line access. In June 1863, rumours of such a line abounded in Caernarfon, but there was no certainty as to where the connection with the network would occur, Caernarfon and Bangor being the most likely options. The contest between these towns began in November 1863 with meetings in support of each route. The Bangor-based *North Wales Chronicle* naturally supported the Bangor and Llanberis Direct Railway (BLDR), emphasising *Direct* and that 'the scheme is so laid out as not to injure private residences, and cause unnecessary severance of property, or to interfere with the ornamental and sporting grounds of the gentlemen through whose property it passes' – a clear nod to the powerful landed interests in the region. As we saw in the previous chapter, any scheme for a railway from Bangor required the support of the Pennant family at Penrhyn Castle to make serious progress. When he took the chair of a meeting in Bangor concerning the scheme, Pennant refused to favour either of the projected lines and claimed that he had not previously known about the Caernarfon scheme. His neutrality was unhelpful to the Bangor line.

The response from Caernarfon was predictably fierce. A meeting convened by the Mayor was heavily attended and the consensus was that the Bangor line would ruin Caernarfon's position as the natural exit route for Llanberis traffic. The Assheton Smith/Duff family of the Vaynol slate empire had none of the neutrality of the Pennants and wrote to the mayor to state that the line from Caernarfon was the best candidate, but 'reserved the right of suggesting any alterations in the line that I might think necessary, where it passes through [our] property'. There was clearly an understanding between the two most powerful families in north Wales that each would not trespass on the interests of the other.

Among other participants in the contest there was greater ferocity and abuse than on any competition for railway projects in north Wales – a high bar. It reached a peak in January 1864 when the Caernarfon interests met in Llanberis and denied access to Bangor supporters, while the Bangor lobby met in Llandinorwig, and ensured that the Caernarfon town crier announced it as an open meeting. The latter meeting suggested that contractors could build both lines and asserted that the one from Bangor would be more successful.

Both parties moved quickly. By the end of February 1864, the BLDR Bill passed a second reading in the House of Lords. It reached committee in March 1864 where Lord Newborough, the Assheton-Smith/Duff family and, crucially, the LNWR opposed it. The LNWR asserted:

> The proposed Railway would interfere with their property in a prejudicial manner, so as to prevent the safe and efficient working of their [CHR], and their carrying on the traffic thereon. That the intended Railway is very badly laid out, its junction with the [CHR] is extremely dangerous, being at the entrance of a cutting 79 feet in depth, and on a curve with a radius of 1 furlong and although it is only 8 miles and 5 furlongs long, it has a gradient of 1 in 80 for nearly 2 miles, and 1 in 55 for one mile of its length. That … it cannot be worked remuneratively or efficiently by an independent Company … That a better scheme than the intended Railway may be devised, and is being promoted, for giving access to Llanberis and providing communication between it and the [CHR] including Bangor.

The committee hearing took copious evidence but faced with the opposition from major landowners and the LNWR, the BLDR's case was hopeless. The *North Wales Chronicle* reported proceedings extensively and in a dramatic 'Stop Press' lamented:

> BY ELECTRIC TELEGRAPH. YESTERDAY (FRIDAY), MARCH 11. Engineering and other evidence was called to-day, and the various Counsels

engaged, addressed their Lordships. The following is the decision of the Committee: — Bangor and Llanberis, and Griffith's Crossing Line thrown out. Decision on Carnarvon Harbour Railway postponed until Monday, to see if the promoters can arrange with the Harbour Trustees for continuation of the Line to the existing [LNWR] Station.

The Carnarvon Harbour scheme – the CLR No 1 – was a variation on the scheme supported by the LNWR. Parliament threw it out, leaving the CLR No 2 scheme as the winner. Caernarfon celebrated this success wildly and took pleasure in reminding Bangor residents of their threat that the BLDR would cause 'grass to grow in the streets of Carnarvon'.

Construction started in September 1864 in Llanberis as did the process by which the LNWR absorbed the line. So, by May 1865 Euston supported the CLR to secure 'powers to work the line and make traffic arrangements with the LNWR'. By September, shareholders heard the construction was on time and that parliament had granted powers to extend the line through Caernarfon to the BCR station.

But construction was not straightforward, as Robert Edwards of Holyhead, 'a member the Wesleyan connection, and much respected by his fellow workmen', discovered in February 1866. In the Llanrug tunnel 'after firing the blast all the men ran to shelter at the farther end of the tunnel, but unfortunately for the deceased, a portion of rock, hurled with tremendous force for about 70 yards, rebounded and struck him on his head ... the poor fellow died [later]'.

In March 1866, the *Caernarvon and Denbigh Herald* noted that LNWR officials had visited Caernarfon and agreed to create a tunnel to connect the CLR with the BCR. The paper saw the uprooting of the poorest residents as an added benefit:

> The irregular mass of small tenements, beneath which huddle together a large proportion of our poverty and immorality, would be swept away, and the breezes from the [Menai] Straits would circulate freely in our streets, without being first polluted by passing through the filthy lanes and alleys of that locality, not altogether inaptly called, Turkey Shore.

The LNWR disingenuously claimed it had never supported the CLR and reckoned it would prefer not to build the tunnel and would only do so if the owners sold them land cheaply. It had the support of the Town Council and the *Caernarvon and Denbigh Herald* and eventually, as usual, got its way. In February 1867, the

LNWR, while reporting to shareholders on an agreement with the CLR, gave an insight into its approach to branch lines that we have seen acted out across north Wales, especially in the 1860s, reported here in the *Morning Herald*:

> For some years past the directors have had to oppose a great number of speculative lines undertaken and projected with a view of trading upon the fears or jealousies of the established companies; [our] policy has steadily been to refuse to purchase these unnecessary lines, believing, as the result has proved, that, if left to their resources, they would collapse. The mischief which this legislation has caused has been felt throughout the kingdom, and a very natural mistrust has thus been engendered in the minds of the public against railways in general.

The less supportive *North Wales Chronicle* preferred to focus on the construction problems of the CLR, but late in 1867 thought things would improve with the application of steam technology in the form of:

> A new locomotive engine, weighing twelve tons, and supplied … by Mr Hughes, Loughborough [the forerunner of Brush engineering] a first-class engine … exceedingly useful in moving materials … [for] construction until the whole length is completed. [Delivering] so heavy and ponderous a piece of machinery was naturally attended with considerable difficulties, and the attempt made on the day of its arrival … turned out a failure. The company then let the affair by contract to Mr Lloyd, Prince of Wales Inn, who has had a good deal of experience with heavy weights; and on Wednesday he engaged a number of men of the right sort, who vigorously set about making the necessary preparations and during that day a great number of persons visited and inspected the new iron horse which is destined to take passengers from Carnarvon to Llanberis in less than half an hour … Twelve powerful horses were yoked to the locomotive which was taken triumphantly through the streets of the town, and on to Cwm-y-Glo, amidst the cheers of large crowds of people. There have been a great many disheartening circumstances connected with the making of this little line, but the chief difficulties have now been surmounted, and doubtless during next spring it will be opened for traffic.

By March 1868, the line was complete as far as Glan Gwna so that 'Carnarvonites can almost hear the music of the iron horse straining away at the ballast trucks', and the *North Wales Chronicle* thought that once it opened it completed the development of railways in north-west Wales. A year later, the opening was still awaited, but the line was in the news in June 1869 because its station at Cwm-y-Glo was badly damaged by an immense explosion of nitro-glycerine carried by horse and cart from Caernarfon docks. Six people died. The explosion diverted attention from the opening of the line early in July 1869 but enabled large crowds to visit the scene giving an early boost to railway revenue. Work continued into August 1869 when Frederick Scott from Devon died after a horse-drawn spoil truck ran him over near the Morfa terminus.

There were intermediate stations on the nine-mile line to Llanberis at Pont Rug, Pontrhythallt and Cwm-y-Glo. There was further non-fatal drama in October when the last coach of a train derailed at Rhug and travelled over a mile before embedding in a wooden bridge at Pontrhythallt ripping up the track before the driver noticed. A report in November 1869 suggested that the LNWR intended to build a 'pick-up' station in Caernarfon below Segontium Terrace and next to Castle Square, though I could find no evidence that it did so.

Carnarvon Morfa station had a brief life until the LNWR created a route under Caernarfon to its own station in 1870. The site of the station is the small dark building to the left of the line. **(LNWR Society)**

Pontrhythallt where a Llanberis train partially derailed and ripped up a long section of track in 1869. This picture from the early 1900s presents a wintery scene in this mountainous district. (WRRC)

By August 1952 Pontrhythallt is past its heyday, as the LMS closed it in 1930, though many features remained. (Online Transport Archive)

Little of the Llanberis branch is visible now but this tunnel between Cwm-y-Glo and the terminus is useful for cyclists and pedestrians to avoid the heavy traffic on the A4086. That road uses some of the route of the old railway. (© Brian Deegan cc-by-sa/2.0)

The most significant event for the LNWR was the connection of the CLR to its network through the new tunnel under Caernarfon. While there was little ceremony when the CLR opened, there was a full turnout of the north Wales gentry and the industrial aristocracy of the LNWR for the connection of all the lines in Caernarfon, and the closure of Pant and Caernarvon Morfa stations that were the termini of the CR and CLR respectively. Chair Richard Moon appeared to suggest in this *Llangollen Advertiser* report that this modern power had overshadowed the landowners when he asserted the LNWR:

Had only accomplished in commerce what they had done in feudalism long ago. They had woven a girdle which now completed the circle round

Shipping interests were unhappy with the arrival of the railway at Caernarfon but the amount of slate on the quayside suggests rail may have added to their business. (John Alsop Collection)

Wales ... they had told their traffic managers that in three years the traffic must be quintupled and if this were realised, it would inaugurate a new era, and increase the wealth and prosperity of the town of Carnarvon.

The quintupling of traffic may have been a factor in the last of the branch developments in this district: the short branch from Penygroes to Nantlle. It attracted little comment with the *Herapath Journal* simply noting in August 1872 that 'the 4 feet 8 inches guage, (sic) between Pen-y-groes and Tal-y-sarn was opened for mineral traffic in May last, when the 3 feet 6 inches guage (sic) was removed; this railway will be ready for passenger traffic in October next' – as indeed it was, with no intermediate stations. This was also the year that stations were added at Ynys and Llangybi. The collapse of the Nantlle wooden goods

Above: Nantlle in 1920 showing the terminus of the short branch from Penygroes that closed in 1932. (John Alsop Collection)

Below: Llangybi station amid a classic rural scene on the Lleyn Peninsula towards the end of it service. It was wilder in 1931 when a freak whirlwind uprooted a signal post. (WRRC)

Above: Dinas Junction connected the LNWR to the North Wales Narrow Gauge Railway which thereby made a small dent in Euston's regional monopoly. (John Alsop Collection)

Below: This north facing view of Dinas Junction in 1910 shows the arrangements for traffic with the North Wales Narrow Gauge Railway joining from behind the camera. (John Alsop Collection)

shed in 1899 showed the basic quality of provision. A goods wagon collided with a supporting pillar, leaving one employee dashing for his life as the structure fell around him.

There was a further branch in 1877 but not one operated by the LNWR. The North Wales Narrow Gauge Railway left the main line south of Caernarfon at the newly created Dinas Junction. The line opened the mountainous interior of north Wales, stopped at the Snowdon Ranger hotel, and aimed to attract tourist and slate traffic.

Moon's ambitions for Caernarfon did not get off to a promising start. In May 1871, a pointsman stored a train on the Llanberis line but forgot about it and there was a serious collision leading to the death of the son of stationmaster Evans. The pointsman absconded. In August 1872, a ballast engine struck the Llanberis market train injuring passengers and damaging rolling stock. Colonel Rich investigated for the Board of Trade, the results being reported in *Railway News*:

> The Quay junction distant signal, next to Carnarvon station, being out of order. [He recommended] that only one train should be allowed to approach this very dangerous junction at the same time [and] the Quay junction home signal should be repeated at the north side of the tunnel towards Carnarvon, and that a signal, locked with the junction signals, should be provided for the siding at the south-east side of Quay junction.

The arrangements for three railways meeting at Caernarfon were clearly inadequate. The various dangers of railway employment were plain from a series of incidents in Caernarfon in 1873. In April, porter Richard Williams, the brother of the Menai Bridge stationmaster, stumbled after the engine driver whistled a warning and died under the train. In November, Alfred Nutt was engaged in shunting operations and fell under moving wagons suffering no injury until he hit his head on the ashpan of the engine. Two accidents occurred nearby in December. Stoker Frederick Broom sustained serious injuries after he stooped from the cab of the moving engine to check the sand pipes and hit his head on a bridge near Turf Square. David Price trapped his head between the buffers of a truck and a stone wall during shunting operations at Caernarfon and was lucky to survive.

The new decade did not start well either, with trainee shunter Thomas Reade (from the Springs Branch railway near Wigan) dying under the wheels of a train at Caernarfon after stumbling. In January 1881, Thomas Jones was injured for a second time within thirteen months when he was clearing snow at Caernarfon and stepped off one track when a train approached into the path of another engine.

Mrs Lloyd-Edwards of Nanhoron (wife of the High Sheriff) saw the unfortunate man on a stretcher and went straight to his house to give a donation to his wife. Some details of the railway arrangements were clear from the death of Hugh Pritchard, a 72-year-old platelayer who died beneath an Afon Wen-bound train in September 1882. He worked in the quay sidings cleaning rails and working the turntable but met his death on the main line near Love Lane and the Seiont bridge. Colleagues had called out and Pritchard heard them but still stepped across the line and under the train, falling 'in the grip' – the water drain by the line. His age seems high for a railway employee, even in the 1880s.

After a brief respite, the pattern continued in 1888 with passenger Morris Thomas killed at Caernarfon station. He tried to board a moving train on a crowded platform and fell under its wheels. Unlike the other incidents noted at Caernarfon, there was criticism of the LNWR for the crowding at the station as a contributory factor. Locals said it was a regular feature made worse on this occasion by the large crowd that had attended to hear the Salvation Army band. A month later near Pont Rug, a Llanberis train derailed, carriages and a bridge were damaged but there were no injuries. John Parry was severely injured when he fell from a Llanberis bound train in December 1894 near Glynrhonwy Quarry.

The new century did not turn the tide of death and injury around Caernarfon. A four-year-old boy died at the Workhouse Crossing (near the old Morfa station) in September 1900, but despite local criticism of the arrangements the coroner proved a stout defender of the LNWR, as can be seen in this *Carnarvon and Denbigh Herald* report:

> The child had wandered along the line, and if the crossing was to be done away with a tunnel or a bridge would have to be constructed, but his opinion was that people rather risked their lives than avail themselves of such advantage. Children, as was well known would go over walls, and no railway company could be expected to keep a policeman to watch every stile.

In 1902, brakesman Hussey fell between wagons during shunting operations and received serious injuries. There was greater shock in July 1903 when two linesmen, James Browne and Henry Owen, died on the track at Turf Square bridge on their way to repair fencing. The engine driver whistled when he saw them, but high winds may have meant that they did not hear the train approaching. There was an elaborate funeral for both men at Glanadda cemetery, Bangor. Again, there was no blame attached to the LNWR at the inquest. In 1907, David Williams was yet another severely injured on shunting duties.

We have seen deaths and injuries on all the branches covered so far but Caernarfon stands out as having a surprising concentration. The events described between 1873 and 1907 involve five deaths and seven injuries to railway staff, with two deaths and one injury to passengers or the public. Even by nineteenth-century standards that seems a high number for a small railway centre in a little over thirty years. Figures for the whole Lleyn Peninsula in the same period would include other incidents such as the fatal smash at Bryncir in 1866.

Apart from Bryncir, the next most serious accident was near Chwilog in 1872, an incident that showed the lax management in this area. A heavily loaded passenger train was returning to Porthmadog from Penygroes after the Eisteddfod. It paused at Chwilog for the customary ticket check, which often occurred on the train just ahead of main stations. The staff at Penygroes took no account of the delay and allowed a second train to leave. This lighter train made rapid progress and smashed into the first train at around 25mph causing 29 serious injuries, but thankfully no deaths.

A lack of lighting in the first train aggravated the incident and made rescue difficult. The inspector's report focused on insufficient brake power on the second train and allowing it to start too soon after the first train. That in turn highlighted the absence of a system of continuous brakes and the absolute block system of signalling. There was thus a gradual move from individual towards corporate responsibility. The LNWR was notably stubborn in adhering to chain braking and slow to adopt block signalling. Remarkably, the application of time interval working was impossible on this occasion because there was no clock at Llangybi station and the stationmaster did not have a working watch.

This period was the peak of 'railway slaughter' in Britain, with a government report by Captain Tyler for 1872 (reproduced in the *Derry Journal*) showing that:

> The number deaths of passengers occurring from accidents over which they have control was only 24, but the total list of killed, including companies' servants, amounted to 1,145; and 3,038 were more or less hurt. Of the killed, 1,018 were servants of the companies—a most significant fact, to which we wish particularly to call attention. No doubt many of these died from accident more or less due to their own recklessness, but these form an insignificant number, compared to that which must laid against a bad system. And those very men who died from their own heedlessness were, Captain Tyler points out, in all probability educated to heedlessness by that system. The greater portion of the railway traffic of the country is carried under needlessly dangerous conditions. It is often a haphazard touch-and-go sort thing, and the men working such system, or no system can hardly fail to grow reckless.

Chwilog saw one of the worst incidents on the branches when two trains collided injuring twenty-nine people in 1872. The station looks serene in the early 1960s as closure approached. **(WRRC)**

The operations of the LNWR in north Wales in this period bear out all Captain Tyler's observations. But as elsewhere in the region, not all incidents resulted from poor management. The presence of stones deliberately placed on the line once again caused derailment, damage, and delay, this time at Ty'n-y-Weirglodd crossing near Penygroes in 1912. In some cases responsibility was highly contested such as when a train killed four cattle at Ynys in 1875 and a furious court case followed in which the farmer argued that the crossing arrangements were poor and the 'special' train, with just one guard's van in tow, was going too fast. For its part, the LNWR insisted that the farmer had been unwise to drive eighteen cattle over the line when a train was due. It argued that he should have known that a fast special was due because the preceding passenger train had a red board attached to its rear coach. I was unable to find the result for this case.

Above and below: Ynys opened in 1872 and in 1875 featured in a court case after cattle died on the station crossing. In 1973 the site was returning to nature nine years after closure. (WRRC)

In 1870 LNWR Chair Richard Moon thought railways could even develop Snowdon. The railway to the summit opened in 1896, the LNWR coordinated services to profit from it and issued this postcard to encourage visits. (Phil Lloyd Collection)

In closing the study of railway branches in this area of north Wales before the end of the nineteenth century, we may briefly note the creation of the Snowdon Mountain Railway, anticipated in Chairman Richard Moon's comment at the opening of the Caernarfon tunnel in 1870 when he suggested that he 'even believed Snowdon was meant to be something more than a place for snow and the clouds to rest upon … railways [will] do very great things for the town and county of Carnarvon'. But it was Moon's rival Sir Edward Watkin who began the process of conquering the peak by acquiring part of the mountain but apparently not considering a railway in 1890. However, the LNWR had an interest with its station at Llanberis, and when the first sod of the new railway was cut in December 1894 it was clear that it would start close to the LNWR station. Contractors completed the line in 1896 but a fatal accident marred its opening when a train left the rails

Llanberis proved to be a popular destination for tourists so that the LNWR profited from extra revenue alongside that from slate traffic. The Snowdon Mountain Railway station is beyond and to the right of the engine shed. (John Alsop Collection)

and fell onto the Llanberis path near Clogwyn. The line was a minor breach of the LNWR monopoly in north Wales, but as usual it managed to turn the event to its own advantage and ran trains to and from Llanberis to link with the Snowdon railway timetable.

The new century opened with the LNWR dominant across north Wales with the small cloud of motor transport still distant. The Investiture of the Prince of Wales at Caernarfon in 1911 was an opportunity to display this power in Wales alongside that of the monarchy. Euston published its own souvenir brochure for the occasion and was at the centre of arrangements for the ceremony. The company did well from the event, as these figures in the *Denbighshire Free Press* demonstrate:

> A special staff of principal collectors have just concluded at Carnarvon the task of counting the bookings to the town in connection with the Investiture.

The figures are as follows: Wednesday, 12,256; Thursday, 20,525; Friday, 4,500; Saturday, 7,272. In addition, the troops, police, sailors, ambulance men, and boy scouts, aggregated 17,250, making a grand total of 61,808.

An even larger task faced the railway with the threat of war. The training camps in north Wales were mostly along the CHR, but Caernarfon had one at Coed Helen in time for the outbreak of war in August 1914, reported here by the *Carnarvon and Denbigh Herald*:

> Fine weather prevailed in Carnarvon on Monday. The holiday mood of the people, however, had in it an element of seriousness, produced by the sudden recall of the East Lancashire and other Territorials, who only got under canvas at Coed Helen the previous day. By one o'clock practically all the troops, numbering about 4,000, had entrained for their respective stations, and this had the result of disorganising the train service for some hours.

By 1915, Caernarfon hosted 15,000 troops supplying a massive traffic for the railway. Loss of staff to army recruitment hampered the LNWR's ability to cope with the influx. As one local correspondent noted in a letter to the *Carnarvon and Denbigh Herald*. 'When the war commenced there were ten cleaners in the engine shed at the station. To-day they are ten soldiers. This is only one instance, and no more can obtain leave to join the Army from the railway, which has already contributed over 70,000.'

In the post-war period, Carnarvonshire County Council criticised the LNWR for its slowness in restoring passenger services, particularly on the Nantlle branch. The LNWR protested that it was doing all that it could. Nantlle services eventually restarted in 1919. Pontrug on the line to Llanberis and Llong on the Chester to Mold line also closed in 1917 and reopened 1919, the former renamed Pont Rug and reduced to the status of a halt in 1920.

Across the Menai Straits, the development of branch lines was less worrying for the LNWR. The only rail route onto Anglesey was over its own BTB which limited any hostile bid to develop lines. The CHR served the south and west of the island, but the focus of that line was the Irish traffic. The most significant industry on Anglesey – the mining of Parys Mountain – was a long way from the line and depended on sea transport. Seaside tourism in Anglesey was small scale compared to mainland north Wales.

Local landed and commercial interests were initially most concerned to secure access to Amlwch and the Parys Mountain. At a meeting in Llangefni in January

There was a large military base in Caernarfon during the First World War and this in turn created a heavy traffic for the railway, as in this 1915 picture. **(John Alsop Collection)**

1863 attendees heard that the project had been around for two years but that it was then ready to go ahead. A notable attendee was R.M. Preston, solicitor to the LNWR and an important figure in Euston's efforts to keep out all competition from north Wales. The lack of local financial commitments to railway projects was a common complaint in north Wales and the Anglesey Central Railway (ACR) was no exception. This meeting heard that the project had raised £16,000 (£1.6million) and that Thomas Brassey and Benjamin Piercy had made generous offers to construct the line and shoulder a large part of the cost. The landowners added to their contribution at the meeting, but there were doubts about Anglesey MP William Owen Stanley's support for their effort, as he was more focused on Holyhead and jealous of any rivalry from Amlwch.

When news of the outcome of the meeting reached Amlwch in January 1863, 'large bonfires were lighted, and a display of fireworks was kept up till a late hour, the inhabitants all evincing the greatest joy at the early prospect they now have of being brought into contact with the outer world.' A month later, Standing Orders

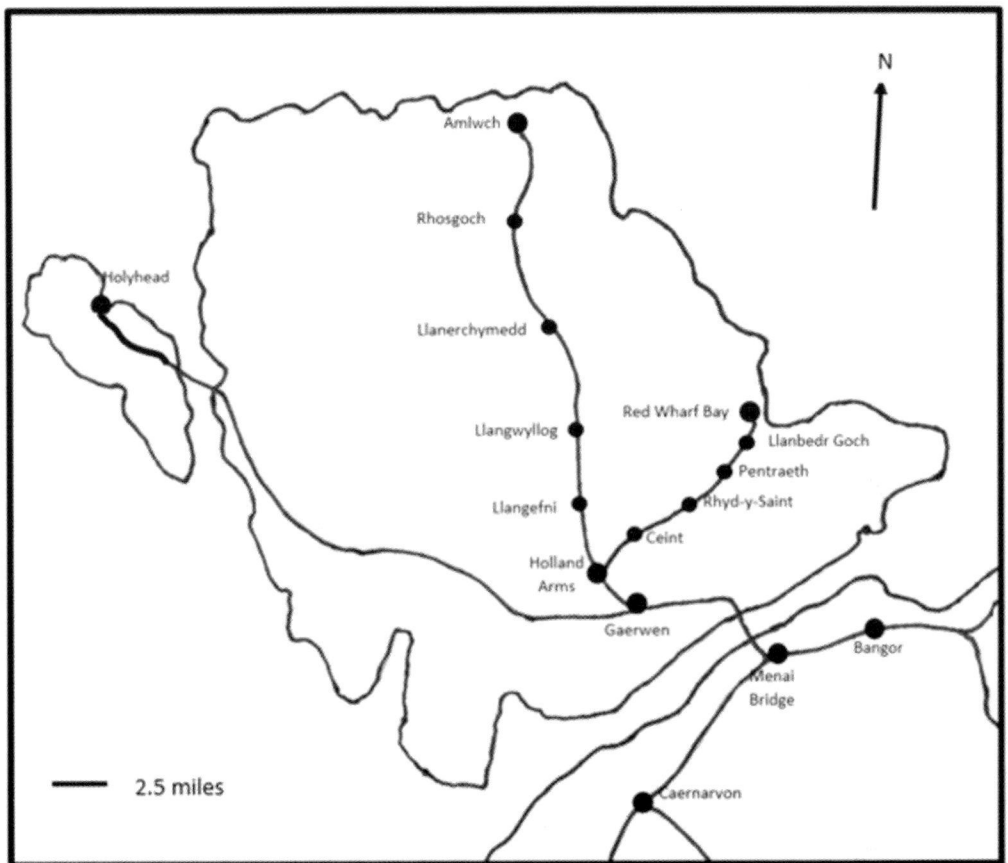

Map 5: Branch lines in Anglesey c 1910.

had been met, by June the Bill was awaiting Royal Assent, and by September the first sod had been cut. Messrs Dickson and Russell constructed the line with Colin Mackenzie as engineer. It was as simple to construct as any branch line in north Wales and was uncontroversial because the LNWR felt no threat to its monopoly. From the start it was clear that the 18 mile line's independence from Euston was nominal. In October, the works between Gaerwen and Llangefni were advanced with the most difficult part being a cutting at Berw Hall, which supplied ballast for the line. There were further heavy works at Ty Mawr near Llangefni where an engine worked alongside forty-five navvies.

In December 1864, the line opened to Llangefni with Martin Smith of the VCR – and prominent in the hostilities in north-east Wales – present as a representative of the LNWR, according to the chair of the gathering. Smith was embarrassed by that connection and tried to sustain the fiction that he was the independent manager of

In 1863 news of the railway caused mass celebrations in Amlwch. Euphoria was in short supply by August 1952 as 2-6-2T 41223 of Bangor shed awaits departure. **(Online Transport Archive)**

the VCR. He then continued in his usual blunt manner to attack the local wealth owners for their unwillingness to risk their money on railways.

Sir Richard Bulkeley, one of the most prominent landowners, saw the railway's arrival as a conquest of the uncivilized as he told the gathering, reported by the *North Wales Chronicle*:

> It was to be hoped the line which was partially opened that day would bring wealth, happiness, and the blessings of civilization and improvement to that county for it went through the very heart of their Island … not until the

Saxons of old got hold of that island were they ever able to hold and to keep possession of the country and this railway now penetrated through its very heart. But though they all must be animated by a degree of love of country, he never saw any country so much in want of civilization as a certain portion of the line through which they came that day.

This was a jaundiced view of the island, which travel-writer George Borrow described in 1856 as 'A place for poets, you meet a poet, or the birthplace of a poet, everywhere'. He also said while touring Anglesey and refusing a ride on the CHR, 'I despise railroads, and those who travel by them' – so he had little in common with Bulkeley.

The April 1865 ACR Board meeting produced too few directors to go ahead, but it heard that progress towards Amlwch was positive, and that the Board of Trade approved the line to Llangefni. The transfer to the LNWR proceeded smoothly by 1866 and in 1867 the inspectors allowed the line to open in June with stations at Holland Arms, Llangefni, Llangwyllog, Llanerchymedd, Rhosgoch and Amlwch. By 1869 the railway had caused the restoration of the market at Amlwch and enabled a substantial Eisteddfod at Llanerchymedd, acknowledged at the event. The ACR experienced poorly attended meetings so that by 1876 it was no surprise that the only quorate Board meeting in London was the one that agreed to sell the line to the LNWR for £80,000 (£7.6million). By 1 July 1876 it was owned by the LNWR.

The ACR directors narrowly avoided being in charge when the most significant railway accident on the island occurred. On 30 November 1877, the 4am mail train left Bangor for Amlwch behind 415 (possibly a Ramsbottom DX goods locomotive) with two coal trucks, a first-class carriage, and a brake van. On board were driver William Taylor, stoker John Saunderson, platelayer John Davies, and guard Edward Hughes. The train paused at Llanerchymedd and had attained 25mph when it reached the site of a wooden bridge that had been washed away by the heavy rain, where it plunged into the swollen river killing all but the guard. Reporting on the events, Colonel Yolland of the Board of Trade found no fault with the management or infrastructure, despite strong local feelings to the contrary, but recommended a better bridge and more protection from flooding of the nearby lake.

Nothing on that scale occurred after 1877 until a notable trio of incidents in 1891. At Holland Arms, a train smashed into the siding buffers and the engine turned over across the main line, being seriously damaged in the process, though thankfully the driver and stoker escaped unhurt. Traffic stopped for seven hours until a breakdown gang from Bangor arrived to clear the line for the evening mail.

D5091 with an Octel train from Amlwch passes the Cefni Reservoir. In November 1877 a freight train derailed in a similar setting after flooding at Llyn Alaw near Llanerchymedd. (Transport Treasury)

Most inconvenienced was a large funeral party heading to Rhosgoch which had to resort to road transport. Signalman and platelayer Richard Williams died at Llanerchymedd station after falling under a train. The *Carnarvon and Denbigh Herald* reported from Llangefni that Jane Williams was 'squeezed in the rush for the train, and in order to save herself caught hold of the handle of a carriage, and was dragged some distance, but was eventually lifted up into the carriage [and was] unconscious for several hours.' Further down the line, in 1894 Henry Simmons, a guard at Llangwyllog station, lost his footing during shunting operations and was killed instantly under the train. In June 1900, a mail train was derailed by stones placed on the line near Amlwch causing extensive damage to the track and long delays to the mail.

Above: *Holland Arms was the junction for the 1909 RWB branch. In this 1962 picture the station had been closed to passengers for ten years.* (John Alsop Collection)

Below: *The sidings at Llanerchymedd in 1905 near where platelayer Richard Williams died under a train in 1891.* (John Alsop Collection)

Jane Williams narrowly escaped death at Llangefni in 1891 after she fell from the crowded platform. This picture shows the station in a quieter phase. (John Alsop Collection)

In contrast to events at Bodfari where there was extensive rioting against efforts to distrain property to pay the tithe to the established church in 1887, there was a more peaceful exercise conducted via Rhosgoch station in 1889 where a low-profile arrival of bailiffs and police enabled collection of the hated tax without the extreme response that had occurred in Denbighshire. A more welcome arrival at the same station was that of local farmer, preacher, soldier and hero Major Owen Thomas of Brynddu on his return from commanding a squadron of Brabant's Horse in the South African war in 1900.

The final addition to the branch line portfolio of the LNWR in this part of north Wales was one that initially attracted little interest from Euston. The light railway movement at the end of the nineteenth century encouraged smaller towns to seek railway connection which spurred the people of east Anglesey to action. In December 1895 there was an extensive meeting of landowners and business

The completion of the station at Amlwch boosted the local economy so that the market in the town returned in 1869. It seems unlikely this picture was on market day. (John Alsop Collection)

people at Pentraeth. It had detailed costings for a railway from the CHR to Red Wharf Bay [RWB] and Benllech, a line for which tourism was the only likely source of income. After considering its options, the meeting decided to petition the LNWR for a standard gauge line to the CHR near Gaerwen. The most influential contributor to the debate was Owen Williams, whose plans helped develop Llandudno in 1845 alongside CHR construction. He suggested Benllech had the potential to match Llandudno but needed a direct rail link. But would the LNWR oblige? One contributor gave his assessment, as reported here in the *Carnarvon and Denbigh Herald*:

> We know that the [LNWR] people are not pioneers. Oh, no; it is a question of £. s. d. with them. But let there be some talk of a (GWR) or any other line, they are very approachable. And I for one feel very happy to-night, because we have two strings to our bow, and we may rest assured that we shall have a railway; because should the [LNWR] refuse us, the Government will give us a light railway.

In the absence of any clear progress by 1897, a consortium led by Theo Rowlands – who claimed to have helped to establish Manchester trams – entered the field with proposals for a network of electric light railways, including Amlwch to Valley, Llanfair PG to Llangoed via Menai Bridge and Beaumaris, and Llangefni through Pentraeth to Red Wharf and Benllech. Over a year later, with no sign of Mr Rowlands and his scheme, the LNWR announced its plans to build a line from Holland Arms to RWB, with the support of local landowners, especially the Vivian family of Plas Gwyn. Contractors marked out the line in July 1900 without ceremony. But by 1902, construction had not started. Likewise in 1904, an editorial in the *North Wales Express* sadly reported:

> There has been talk for years of running a branch of the Anglesey line from Holland Arms via Pentraeth. The topic is always conversationally fresh in the district, which proves that both inhabitants and visitors, though balked of their desire so long, have yet some faith in the railway authorities.

That faith evaporated in 1905 with news that the LNWR would introduce buses instead, even though it had deposited railway building materials at Holland Arms. A year later work started, and a large army of navvies was in the area. This intrusion was uncaring of the ancient history of Anglesey:

> The steam navvy is now ruthlessly tearing its way through the Myrddyn Gwyn tumulus, near Pentraeth, which lies in the way of the track ... and any archaeological treasure unearthed by the machine's resistless bite is foredoomed to fracture. As far as possible, however, a look out is being kept, and if anything is disclosed that can be saved intact, willing hands will strive to rescue it. The other day an urn was brought to light but was destroyed by the steam navvy, though some of the fragments were secured.

The line eventually opened in May 1909 with a low-key ceremony led by local traffic manager L.A.P. Warner. The line was 7 miles long with stations at Ceint, Rhyd-y-Saint, Pentraeth, Llanbedr Goch and RWB and Benllech, though stopping short of the coast. The report in the *Carnarvon and Denbigh Herald* captured the sense that the LNWR had little enthusiasm for the line but had tired of the pressure for more railways in Anglesey:

> The railway company ran the risk of much loss if they acceded to the demand for a branch railway to any of the places claiming one; the claimants ran no risk at all. Clamour carried the day, and the [LNWR] decided to construct a branch railway to *somewhere*. [my emphasis]

There were few incidents, but the court fined David Lewis after the police ejected him from Llanbedr Goch station for drunkenness and molesting passengers in 1910.

The line irritated the increasing national awareness in Wales in its decision to use Anglicised versions of Welsh placenames. This was not the first time the railways had done this, but it provoked a more general complaint that reflected the growth in national awareness, as the *North Wales Times* pointed out:

> There is no place more objectionable than the watering place hastening to forget its Welsh life and to adopt a kind of [corrupted] English life and language instead ... who tamely submit to have the names of the villages they live in ruined and vulgarised by such changes as ... Traeth Coch to 'Red Wharf' ... We hope that the day is coming when it will be realised how infinitely nobler are the old life and the old ideals than the mean and vulgar life that too often takes their place.

By 1914 Anglesey had a good road around it and the LNWR supplied buses linked to trains including motor trains on the Red Wharf branch. As noted in the *North Wales Chronicle*, 'The ... new services should go a long way to ensure for the island a larger population and greater prosperity within the next few years.'

Four days later the country went to war so that the efforts of the LNWR to secure a return on its investments in Anglesey were frustrated. The LNWR memorial book issued to the families of all employees killed in the war listed twenty-one men employed on the branch lines. These were mostly in roles such as porter, guard, cleaner or underman. Llandudno suffered four deaths, Caernarfon and Mold three each, Denbigh and Deganwy two each, Llanberis, Bodfari, Blaenau Ffestiniog,

Above: Llanbedr-Goch station had only basic facilities in 1909 for this quiet backwater. David Lewis intruded on this peaceful scene through drunkenness and molesting passengers here a year later. (John Alsop Collection)

Below: There is a big welcome for the first train at Pentraeth in July 1909 after many years waiting for a rail service. It lost porter Freddie Weeks to the war in 1917. (John Alsop Collection)

Above: RWB and Benllech has a varied collection of well-dressed passengers in this early picture. (John Alsop Collection)

Below: All quiet at RWB and Benllech station on a damp day. The station served neither of its named places effectively due to its location. (John Alsop Collection)

L. & N. W. RAILWAY

VISIT THE

ISLE OF ANGLESEY.

THROUGH SERVICE of TRAINS with MANCHESTER

		a. m.			a. m.
EXCHANGE STATION	dep.	11 30	HOLYHEAD	dep.	10 35
		p. m.	VALLEY	"	10 44
BANGOR	arr.	1 58	RHOSNEIGR	"	10 54
MENAI BRIDGE	"	2 15	TY CROES	"	11 00
GAERWEN	"	2 20	AMLWCH	"	10 30
HOLLAND ARMS	"	2 55	RHOSGOCH	"	10 37
(Change for Red Wharf Bay Line)			LLANERCHYMEDD	"	10 44
CEINT	"	3 5	RED WHARF BAY	"	10 10
RHYD-Y-SAINT	"	3 8	LLANBEDRGOCH	"	10 12
PENTRAETH	"	3 15	PENTRAETH	"	10 16
LLANBEDRGOCH	"	3 19	RHYD-Y-SAINT	"	10 23
RED WHARF BAY	"	3 21	CEINT	"	10 26
LLANERCHYMEDD	"	3 10	HOLLAND ARMS	"	11 7
RHOSGOCH	"	3 25	GAERWEN	"	11 22
AMLWCH	"	3 35	MENAI BRIDGE	"	11 33
BODORGAN	"	2 39			p. m.
TY CROES	"	2 45	EXCHANGE STATION ARR.		3 8
RHOSNEIGR	"	2 49			
VALLEY	"	2 59			

Through trains also leave Exchange for Holyhead at 10:45 a.m. 3-40 p.m., 9.30 p.m., 10.45 p.m.

Through trains also leave Holyhead at 12-0 noon and 5.30 p.m. for Manchester.

Passengers to and from Ceint, Rhyd-y-Saint, Pentraeth, Llanbedrgoch, and Red Wharf Bay change at Holland Arms.

TOURIST TICKETS ISSUED DAILY BY ANY TRAIN

WEEK-END, SHORT AND LONG DATE TICKETS issued every FRIDAY AND SATURDAY by any train.

Write for illustrated guides, programmes etc.

On receipt of a postcard bearing reference Z125 Mr. C Lowndes, District Superintendent, Exchange Station, Manchester will be pleased to supply all information.

Euston Station, London, July 1909

Figure 1: Euston made an impressive attempt in Manchester to publicise the line to RWB soon after it opened. (Copy created by the author)

Rhydymwyn and Betws-y-Coed one each – and one direct impact on the Red Wharf line as Freddie Weeks, a porter at Pentraeth, was killed in action in France in 1917. Two Caernarfon men won the Military Medal, a Mold porter the Meritorious Service Medal and M.D. Orr from Ruthin was mentioned in despatches but died early in 1919. At Ceint, a report praised the line for creating access to historic Plas Penmynydd where the Tudor dynasty started, and where in 1915 the *North Wales Chronicle* reporter reflected on how war had changed the workforce and how the owner was 'a true type of what a woman worker should be'.

In this chapter we have explored the development of branches in north-west Wales. For a time, the competition was fierce as the LNWR struggled with those trying to create the 'third force' in Welsh railways and build a port to compete with Holyhead. As in the rest of the region, the LNWR proved too large and too wealthy for competing railway concerns or the ancient landowning families, and by 1870 had a virtual monopoly in north Wales, as Richard Moon crowingly told those gathered to celebrate the tunnel under Caernarfon in 1870. In Anglesey, the monopoly of the crossing to the island meant that the LNWR had no concern about rival railways and bought the ACR in a leisurely manner. The need to take account of local feelings induced Euston to create a branch to RWB in 1909 but that was a minor development to appease local feeling. The war and the motor vehicle were much larger concerns for the company so that when war ended and the LNWR faced its own demise, the branch lines were especially vulnerable.

Chapter 6
The Decline of the North Wales Branch Lines

'Deep incisive, antiseptic; amputative surgery on the grand scale.'
Commons Debate 30 April 1963

We have seen the growth of a branch line network in north Wales from the opening of the CHR in 1848 to the final branch to Holywell in 1912. In this chapter we will see it unravelling in little more than half that time. The development of branches occurred in distinct periods and so did closure. It began with rationalisation after the First World War in the face of road transport competition, a similar process after the Second World War and then a gradual acceleration through the 1950s leading eventually to the 'Beeching Axe' which tends to be shorthand for railway closures. The reality in north Wales is that Beeching merely finished a job that started in earnest with the 1953 Transport Act.

The First World War caused a temporary loss of services at Nantlle, Pont Rug and Llong. It also accelerated a change that started before the war ended, according to this *North Wales Weekly News* article of January 1917:

> The withdrawal of railway excursion tickets from the coast resorts to Carnarvon, Llanberis, Bettws-y-Coed, Festiniog, Portmadoc, and the other stations to which in ordinary times the visitors flocked in order to see the more famous places in North Wales or to climb the better-known mountains of the Cambrian range, led to an increased demand for seats on the motor charabancs, by which tours from the principal resorts could be made through picturesque North Wales.

Despite this emerging threat from road transport, local authorities continued to debate the 'Light Railway Question' in 1919 and demanded more lines such as one from Wrexham to Ruthin, which was originally suggested in the 1850s. There was one significant addition to the network, the Welsh Highland Railway (WHR) from Dinas Junction to Porthmadog in June 1923 linking two of the four big railways that emerged from the rationalisation of the national system implemented in the same year. The London Midland and Scottish Railway (LMS) replaced the LNWR and the GWR absorbed Cambrian Railways. The Liberal Welsh Nationalist Beriah Gwynfe Evans cited the WHR, reported here by the *Western Mail*, as evidence of a bright future for the economy of north Wales – a 'virgin field of mineral wealth':

> To bring the produce of the quarries to the market the [slate] industry depends entirely upon two railway corporations enjoying a monopoly of the Welsh slate trade … This monopoly is now on the point of being broken by the [WHR] which, linking up with the Festiniog Toy Railway at Portmadoc, introduces a new factor into the tourist and transport facilities of Snowdonia proper. The [WHR] enjoys what Wales as a national entity now demands, absolute autonomy. Bounded, hemmed in on all sides by the two giant railway corporations, the little [WHR] maintains complete independence.

Evans's wider analysis was correct about the gradual replacement of coal by oil, about hydro-electric power and the immense growth in tourism, all of which he saw helping north Wales and potentially causing it to become the centre of a new Welsh state, as it had been in medieval times. His analysis was weaker when it emphasised the need to break the LNWR/GWR domination to release the potential of the region and seeing the WHR as being capable of doing so.

So, his optimism was unfounded. Road traffic had already weakened the LNWR/GWR duopoly by 1923 and in 1936 the WHR ceased trading. In practice, from 1923 all railways in north Wales struggled to prosper and lost ground continually to the burgeoning carriage of people and goods by road. The war had worn out the railways, leaving them poorly placed to respond. That pressure was most marked on branch lines.

There was, of course, a national context, notably that the national economy shrank in the period 1919-26 and again during 1930-31. By 1928 there was increasing comment about the drag on railway profitability caused by branch lines, including one by author and playwright Samuel Bensusan, writing to the *Daily News* in 1928:

> [We have seen] the steady supersession of the small branch railway line, to the little [combustion] engine which, like a wounded snake, drags its slow length along, carrying its beggarly array of empty benches in the service of no useful purpose. Only the goods trains look to be solvent. Do not our railway authorities possess sufficient vision to realise that the branch line

is as dead as Queen Anne, that road transport has dealt the death blow, and that shareholders are maintaining the corpse? In the interests of sound finance and possible dividends the unprofitable local lines should be shut down. A single motor bus would do the entire work of many a rural line train at a fraction of the expense, and to the complete satisfaction of the traveller.

It is a reasonable guess that Bensusan held railway shares.

As if to answer Bensusan's criticisms, Sir Ralph Wedgwood, Chief General Manager of the London and North Eastern Railway, noted in 1929:

It almost a commonplace to refer to the closing of branch lines, and some enthusiasts see them turned into motor roads. It would probably cost more to turn a railway into a road than to make a new road altogether, but ... it is probable that the abandonment of branch lines will not go ... as far as is anticipated.

Wedgewood understood that closures would be unpopular, even when replaced by a bus service and noted that roads would be unable to deliver coal, timber, and other heavy traffic. He granted that some branch passenger services would end but preferred to see companies cut costs by changes such as using motor coaches and light engines and he wondered whether 'local authorities, rather than see railway services abandoned, will be prepared to pay for their continuance' – again predicting a future trend.

In north Wales, the LMS was determined to take on the daunting challenge. One of its managers told a business conference in Rhosneigr in 1933 that 'railways are not dying'. He reported the LMS had carried 117 million tons of freight and 407.5 million passengers in 1932 and was speeding up trains and making other changes to ensure its rail network survived.

How did those changes affect north Wales? Within the first six months of its existence the LMS slashed the cost of carrying groceries to north Wales from Liverpool and Manchester so that:

Railway rates now in force are substantially lower than [those of] the wholesale grocers by several shillings per ton, and the result must inevitably mean increased carryings by the [LMS] who have recently extended their delivery services in North Wales, and considerably improved their transit arrangements.

It reorganised Llandudno station into a 'closed station' (controlled access to platforms) by erecting strong gates and creating a larger concourse to manage the huge crowds of visitors.

By the end its first year, the LMS had enlisted the services of notable artists, whose posters adorned its stations and would, it hoped, boost tourist traffic to the region. Between 1935 and 1939 the LMS had camping coaches at branch line stations including Bethesda, Brynkir, Dyserth, Llanberis, Nantclwyd, Pont-y-Pant, Rhuddlan, Roman Bridge and Tregarth. Halts opened on the Dyserth branch at St Melyd Golf Links and Allt-y-Graig in 1923 and 1928, respectively. The LMS also provided services across north Wales for special occasions such as the Royal Agricultural Show at Chester in 1925. The speed of services also improved in the region in 1926 as noted in the advertisement in Figure 2. And more trains to Denbigh, Ruthin and Blaenau Ffestiniog ran from 1933.

The LMS developed fully integrated road and rail transport in 1928:

A striking example of the energy with which the railways are meeting the competition of the roads will be furnished by a great scheme which the [LMS] is putting into operation in North Wales. It consists in the organisation of a system of road motor services designed to facilitate the transport of goods and parcels traffic throughout the whole area from Chester to Holyhead. Railhead distribution on these lines has been applied before to isolated places, but never until now to a whole area, as in this case.

The scheme centred on Mold, Betws-y-Coed, Holywell Junction, Penygroes, Llandudno Junction, Llanrwst, Ruthin, Caernarfon, Abergele, Llangefni, Denbigh, Bangor, Rhyl, and Valley (Anglesey). From these centres motor services radiated to 'every hamlet and village in the area'. LMS interest in road transport went further in 1929 during which chair Sir Josiah Stamp told the LMS AGM about proposed legislation through which:

The company seek powers to provide passenger and goods services on the publicly owned roads in any district to which access is afforded to their systems, either by themselves or by agreement with other road users, [that] enables them to apply their funds for the purposes of such services and agreements in the interests of the general public and of the railway shareholders.

L M S

TRAIN SERVICE

NORTH WALES COAST

and branches

Commencing Monday September 20th, 1926

THE LOCAL TRAIN SERVICES
BETWEEN

Chester and Rhyl,	Chester and Denbigh,
Rhyl and Llandudno Jct.,	Denbigh and Corwen,
Llandudno Jct. and Bangor,	Mold and Brymbo,
Bangor and Holyhead,	Rhyl and Denbigh,
Prestatyn and Dyserth,	Llandudno Jct. and Blaenau Ffestiniog,
Bangor and Bethesda,	Bangor and Carnarvon,
Carnarvon and Afonwen,	Carnarvon and Llanberis,
Gaerwen and Amlwch.	Holland Arms and Red Wharf Bay.

and the Llandudno and Colwyn Bay Rail Motor Service

WILL BE ACCELERATED

For details of services and Cheap Fare arrangements apply at Stations.

H. G. BURGESS

General Manager

Figure 2: The LMS accelerated services in north Wales in September 1926. (Copy created by the author)

After a fierce debate, parliament granted powers and the LMS bought the Crosville Motor Company in 1929 – a large bus operator in north Wales which had regularly paid a 10 per cent dividend –at a cost of almost £400,000 (£21 million).

This purchase reinforced, rather than refuted, the idea that road transport was gaining ground on the railways, especially in the provision of local services. In September 1930, the LMS announced a series of closures as it rationalised its network. In north Wales, the LMS closed the short-lived branch to Red Wharf and Benllech and its five stations, although the station at Holland Arms continued. The shortest lifespan was for the new halts on the Dyserth branch that closed with the rest of the line in this cull. The Llanberis branch lost its stations, though the branch continued to cater for seasonal traffic with the benefit of a new halt at Padarn, close to the centre of Llanberis from 1936. Surprisingly, Nantlle survived in 1930, but it was a brief respite as the station closed in August 1932, so that fifteen passenger stations closed in this process, around 17 per cent of the total. It is hard to criticise the LMS for its actions. Trading conditions were difficult and there is no doubt that the new company made strenuous efforts to compete with (and integrate) road transport. But the peak of the railway age had passed.

Despite closure in in 1930, Llanberis continued to cater for excursions such as in August 1952. **(Online Transport Archive)**

L M S

SPECIAL NOTICE

PADARN HALT (LLANBERIS) WILL BE OPEN EACH SATURDAY COMMENCING NOVEMBER 21st AND THE FOLLOWING EXCURSION

TRAINS WILL CALL

To Caernarvon and Bangor - Padarn Halt depart:-

| 10.22 a.m. | 12.32 p.m. | 2.12 p.m. |
| 3.32 p.m. | 5.2 p.m. | 7.12 p.m. |

To Padarn Halt:

Bangor Depart: Caernarvon Depart;

| 1.8 p.m. | 3.50 p.m. | 6.11 p.m. | 1.36 p.m. | 4.10 p.m. | 6.35 p.m. |
| 8.30 p.m. | 10.20 p.m. | 11.15 p.m. | 8.55 p.m. | 10.45 p.m. | 11.45 p.m. |

The excursion Fares Advertised from Llanberis will apply from Padarn Halt

(696)

Figure 3: LMS innovations include opening new halts such as Padarn in 1936. (Copy created by the author)

The Dyserth branch supplies a case study of the changes in north Wales, and elsewhere. The popularity of the line with commuters and tourists grew quickly after its opening in 1905, with 1,750 travelling on one day during a damp Whitsuntide holiday in 1909, and with its four stations in just 3.25 miles it was easily accessible. Innovations such as motor trains also helped this branch.

The arrival of war in 1914 changed the outlook. The trains continued to run but the company neglected maintenance, so reliability declined. As we have seen, the LMS tried hard to increase use of the line with added halts but had to admit defeat in 1930. The reflections of the *Prestatyn Weekly* in September on the closure showed the shift in public mood – a certain nostalgia and an acceptance of technological change:

There was a sense of nostalgia for the old 'Mountain Railway' when the Dyserth branch closed to passengers in 1930, but also a sense of the inevitable as road transport advanced. (John Alsop Collection)

Many people will regret the discontinuance of the local passenger train from Prestatyn to Meliden and Dyserth, which puffed along the single line up the Hillside for the last time on Saturday night and steamed back again into the Prestatyn Station to discharge its last human load upon the tiny platform. One has a sentimental regard for an institution that has performed useful service … and it is with a feeling of genuine regret that we bid farewell to the little train which has made its final journey along the mountain side … It is a reversion to the old order. Unsatisfactory road locomotion caused the little train to be started. And a remarkable transformation in the conveniences offered to travellers along our public highways has resulted in its stoppage. It is significant of one thing, and that is the extreme popularity of road travel over that by railway ... And so far, the buses have kept splendidly to time ... There is no doubt that [the LMS are] doing their utmost to render the best possible service to those affected by the stoppage of the train, in a few months all departments of the system will be in satisfactory order.

The rest of the decade saw few further closures, though Griffiths Crossing went in 1937 and Padarn Halt in 1939. The shed at Caernarfon closed in September 1931 and thirty staff moved, mostly to Bangor.

The public accepted these losses, as the tone of the *Prestatyn Weekly* comment above suggests. And Hansard affords few examples of parliamentary interest in the branch lines of north Wales after the First World War. Caernarvonshire MP Goronwy Owen used a bid for more powers by the LMS in March 1927 to raise the 'condition of ... Dolgarrog Station, where ... there is a small shed, but practically no other convenience, and in very inclement weather scores of people get wet [while at Port Dinorwic] several people have experienced injuries as the result of the inadequate arrangements for lighting the platform.' There was no parliamentary comment about the substantial closures in 1930, but it is perhaps not coincidental that they occurred during an extensive break in parliamentary sittings.

A report in 1937 showed the continued potential of the branch lines and the strenuous efforts of the LMS to accommodate customers. The Williams brothers of Frank Farm near Coed Talon station decided to sell up and move to Anglesey. They asked the LMS to arrange the move, and the company did so perfectly via Denbigh, Rhyl, Bangor and Gaerwen. Large crowds saw the operation at both ends. The train left at 9.10am and staff completed the job by 2.15pm:

> The efficiency of the [LMS] in dealing with this matter deserves the highest praise for the whole removal was carried out between feeding and milking time for the cattle, further single line working was necessary at both forwarding and receiving points and the service was carried out without the slightest difficulty ... the composition of the removal were 2 containers, household effects, 33 cattle; 6 calves; 3 horses; approximately 20 pigs; fowl; ducks and geese, farm implements of every description; passengers and feeding stuffs.

There were few incidents and accidents on the well-kept branch lines that survived the closures. One at Holywell Town gave an insight into its working arrangements. In July 1925, the driver left the footplate at the rear to control the speed of the

Coed Talon is a hive of activity around Stanier Class 4, 42461 2-6-4T in this picture from a tour in October 1955, after the station closed to passengers in 1950. It would have been similarly busy when the LMS moved the owners, their possessions, and animals from nearby Frank Farm to Anglesey in 1937. **(WRRC)**

train from the front, while the stoker stayed to keep up steam pressure and braking. Unknown to the driver, the fireman fell off the footplate so that the train hit the buffers at Holywell Town causing significant damage to it and injury to the crew. There was gloom in the close-knit railway colony at Saltney Ferry (Mold Junction) when William Allen was hit and killed by an express at the station as he crossed the main line to help refuel an engine. The derailment at Star Crossing of a special train taking Sunday School children from Mold to Rhyl in 1934 caused temporary alarm in the district but no injuries, and it proceeded just two hours late for the trip.

Llandudno featured prominently in mishaps. In 1923, a train from there smashed into the gates of the level crossing just north of Llandudno Junction. The most serious incident occurred in 1925 at Llandudno station when the motor train to Colwyn Bay left the station against the signal just as a steam-hauled train arrived. The driver of the latter train was alert to the danger and speeded up so that the collision was to the side of the train and not head-on. Remarkably, father and son drove the trains. Jeremiah Pritchard drove the motor train and was quite severely injured as were sixteen passengers, many of them school children. His son Robert in the other train prevented a much more serious incident.

At the enquiry, Jeremiah Pritchard explained that he usually moved forward from the platform and waited at the signal to avoid latecomers jumping aboard the train. On this occasion, he had a brief conversation with the guard about the need to stop at Conwy which he thought had distracted him. He sat while giving evidence but rose to his feet to make a final and commendable statement. 'I hope you won't blame the guard. I would rather be punished as a man who has made a mistake than be liberated as a liar. Whatever I have said, I think I have said the whole truth. I take all the blame.' Also at Llandudno in August 1930, a crowded train from Manchester smashed into the buffers injuring seventeen people. One of the injured recovered quickly as his broken leg was wooden and the staff arranged an immediate repair. In July 1939, there was a similar crash at the station which injured sixteen passengers.

Many incidents were not the fault of the railway, though a spark from an engine set fire to a plantation adjacent to Ynys station in 1925 which then ignited the bone-dry peat and continued to burn with huge clouds of smoke for a fortnight. In January 1925, the line was flooded at Dolgarrog after heavy rain, but not nearly so badly as in November that year when the Eigiau dam burst and destroyed a significant part of the village with many casualties. The road from the station to the village closed to prevent the many ghoulish visitors to the scene arriving by rail.

Two boys pushed a luggage truck off the platform in front of an excursion train returning to Ruthin from Blackpool at Llong in in 1931 damaging the engine. At Afon Wen in 1936, teacher Thomas Langshaw was with a party of schoolchildren on a camping holiday. Staff told the children to use the bridge when crossing the railway but inexplicably Mr Langshaw chose to cross the line directly and a train hit him. No blame attached to railway arrangements or officials, but the coroner and jury criticised the primitive arrangements for storing Mr Langshaw's body at Afon Wen station pending the inquest.

There was a serious snow drift that affected the Afon Wen–Caernarfon branch in February 1928 and was reported in the *Sheffield Independent*:

[One train] ran into a dense bank of snow about two miles from Penygroes. The blizzard had piled up the snow to a height of from six feet to eight feet along

Llong closed for two years from 1917 but survived after reopening until 1962 with some minor excitement. In 1931 boys pushed a luggage truck in front of a Blackpool excursion train returning to Mold. **(LNWR Society)**

the track. Hours later, after several attempts to release the engine, the driver notified the stationmaster at Penygroes, who took to the scene sandwiches and hot tea for the passengers, who numbered about thirty. A platelayer's hut was thrown up and a fire was lighted, and here the travellers found a welcome shelter. Most of them were children who attend Carnarvon School.

Even worse drifts existed beyond Pant Glas station, an engine from Afon Wen being held up in one of them all night. A third mishap occurred on the Nantlle branch line, when an engine to which a coach was attached ran into a drift. The passengers had to leave and take to the road [leaving the engine] imprisoned by the ice and snow.

Three years later a freak whirlwind destroyed the signal at Llangybi station. Less serious was a mailbag robbery between Prestatyn and Dyserth a few weeks before the line closed to passengers in 1930. Five years later, a truck was derailed between Llangefni and Llanerchymedd causing the use of an early rail replacement bus. The lack of incidents was reflected in the national figure given in 1929 of one passenger death for every 36 million miles travelled by train. On the roads of north Wales by contrast, the death toll was horrendous. The loss of life reached its height during the Second World War when, despite traffic reduction, 482 people died and there were 6,000 injuries in the region, far higher than the 'railway slaughter' of the 1870s discussed earlier.

There was little to report on the branch lines of north Wales during the war, and censorship meant less information was available than in the 1914-18 conflict, so that the secret store of mustard gas at Rhydymwyn did not emerge until after the war was over. Railways issued general statements such as in January 1940 when the LMS reported it had broken records for the carriage of goods – 520,600,00 loaded wagon miles in the first four months of the war, an increase of 21.65 per cent. Little of that would have been on the north Wales branches, but the demands on the railway and the reduction in car use meant that the issue of branch line closures disappeared for the duration. At Llandudno, the extensive use of female labour showed the changes and attitudes of the times, chronicled in the *North Wales Weekly News*:

> A woman who wore blue overalls under her coat, and who had just trundled a goods laden truck along one of the platforms at Llandudno railway station, told our reporter that the work was not so tiring as being a waitress. Women have been employed by the [LMS] for about a month … They work the same hours as the men, and the men acknowledge that they are 'pulling their weight.' … 'Don't you feel the cold?' one of the women was asked. 'Not a bit,' she replied. 'I have never felt better. The outdoor exercise gives me an enormous appetite.'

She added that the pay was useful but did not specify whether it was the same as the men. Almost certainly not.

Less creditable was the behaviour of some troops in Llandudno as the war neared its end. The court fined Gunner Harry Fisher £1 (£35) for travelling on the roof of a south bound train near Deganwy, where he hit his head on the footbridge and fell to the ground. He had climbed on the roof in response to a drunken dare and remembered nothing of the incident until after he recovered at Broad Green hospital in Liverpool.

That incident occurred close to a notable tragedy in February 1940 when infant James McClure wandered away from his father who was moving wastepaper on Deganwy Quay. A train hit James near the level crossing. Mr McClure pointed out the absence of proper fencing on the railway, but the coroner chose to emphasise the lack of attention of Mr McClure, no doubt adding to the poor man's distress.

> **VITAL AND URGENT**
>
> A situation may arise at any time in which railways would be unable, for an indefinite period, to accept certain traffic, including fertilisers.
>
> **ORDER YOUR FERTILISERS NOW**
>
> **OR YOU WON'T GET THEM**

ISSUED BY THE MINISTRY OF AGRICULTURE AND FISHERIES

Figure 4: Warning issued to farmers in 1944. (Copy created by the author)

In September 1940, Evan Hughes from the LMS signalling department was moving timber near Afon Wen and died under a train that his colleague said they did not hear because of the high winds. In the same area in 1944, a goods truck became detached from its train and descended the slope towards Afon Wen at speed. The signal operator directed it to a siding where it smashed through a stop-block and ended up in a ditch.

The strain on the railways during the war is clear from a series of small advertisements issued towards the end and in the first period of peace. Newspapers published one that was particularly relevant to farmers on the rural branch lines in February 1944 shortly before the invasion of France, as seen in Figure 4.

Towards the end of the war, the railway companies argued for a different approach to railway funding, particularly a recognition of the light costs borne by road carriers compared to railways. Figures showed that railways used one-third of receipts for maintenance and investment while only one-eighth of the receipts of road carriers contributed to roads and other infrastructure through tax. The companies suggested that full nationalisation was not the answer, but the state could take over the infrastructure and charge for access – foreseeing a later direction in railway policy. As we have seen, the war had taken its toll but gave the railways a temporary life-support. Some thought the railways were already in serious trouble in 1939, having struggled to invest and compete with road traffic and raided funds reserved for improvement to pay dividends.

THE RAILWAYS ARE SHORT OF TRAINED STAFF

Nearly 100,000 skilled railwaymen, one-sixth of the staff, have still to be demobilised. When they return their skills and services will be available to the public
In the meantime, this shortage may affect YOUR train.

TO RESTORE
PRE-WAR STANDARDS
WILL TAKE TIME

GWR • LMS • LNER • SR

THE RAILWAYS ARE SHORT OF LOCOMOTIVES

For six years locomotives have worked hard. Now they are showing signs of the continuous strain
That is why, every day more than 3,000 locomotives are undergoing or awaiting overdue repair.
This daily shortage may affect YOUR train.

TO RESTORE
PRE-WAR STANDARDS
WILL TAKE TIME

GWR • LMS • LNER • SR

THE RAILWAYS ARE SHORT OF CARRIAGES

Every day 3,500 war-worn carriages – one-eighth of the total stock —are taken out of action
Some undergoing repair. Others must await attention because skilled labour and materials are not fully available
This daily shortage of 100,000 seats may affect YOUR train.

TO RESTORE
PRE-WAR STANDARDS
WILL TAKE TIME

GWR • LMS • LNER • SR

THE RAILWAYS ARE SHORT OF LOCOMOTIVE COAL

Like other industries, the Railways are affected by the national fuel shortage.
Like the housewife, the Railways are having to use coal of inferior quality.
The shortage of suitable coal may affect YOUR train.

TO RESTORE
PRE-WAR STANDARDS
WILL TAKE TIME

GWR • LMS • LNER • SR

Figure 5: February and March 1946 the local papers – as in this example in the North Wales Weekly News – in north Wales told readers to expect an impact from a range of national issues affecting railways. (Copy created by the author)

These arguments concluded for a time when government chose to nationalise the railways and on 1 January 1948 BR was born, to the amusement of the *North Wales Weekly News*:

> The railways of this country became the British Railways (BR) ... there appears to have been little to mark the change in North Wales. Exception: the railway porter at Llandudno station who on New Year's Day wore a bowler hat marked ... with the letters "BR", a crown and a device which was suspiciously like a snail rampant.

And for the remaining period of the post-war Labour government there was little change to the branch lines in north Wales, though Coed Talon, Llanfynydd, and Brymbo stations closed in March 1950. Llanfynydd almost burned down after fire broke out in the waiting room in 1947 and staff had difficulty controlling the blaze because of burning oil and exploding fog detonators. Dinas Junction closed in September 1951.

The arrival of the Conservative government in October 1951 heralded a notable change. The broad aim of the 1947 Transport Act was to integrate all forms of transport and require them in aggregate to break even. The 1953 Act denationalised road transport, restored competition with the railways, and left the latter to cover its debts while keeping the financial burden of being a common carrier. A key government argument was that Labour had paid too much for the railways and burdened them with interest debt. In opposition, Labour pointed out that this was the reverse of the argument used by Churchill for the Conservatives on nationalisation, that the government had robbed the private companies by paying too little.

Even before the act took effect, the line to Bethesda lost its passenger services in 1951 as did Holland Arms in 1952. These were minor changes that attracted little criticism. The first major loss of mileage since 1930 was in February 1953 with the end of passenger services between Ruthin and Corwen and the loss of four stations. Again, it drew little comment perhaps because the line offered a sparse service – six south bound trains a day in 1950 – and so was little relied on by local people. The closure came just too late to save stoker Palmer who died when his head hit a bridge in August 1952 as the local train from Denbigh to Corwen approached Eyarth.

More meaningful changes began with the 1954 Modernisation Plan that aimed to increase the use of diesel and electric trains, supply better track and signalling and more automation. MPs expected closures, especially as the British Transport

Eyarth station closed in February 1953. Fireman Palmer may have been the last fatality on this line when he hit his head on a bridge near here in August 1952. (WRRC)

Llanfynydd almost burned down in 1947 and closed in 1950. In LNWR days, employees pose in front of an oil train. (LNWR Society)

Heavy snow affected Pant Glas in 1928 – unlike this pleasant summer scene as the closure of the line approaches. Surprisingly, there are signs of building work on the platform. **(LNWR Society)**

Commission Report in 1954 showed rural branch lines as a major source of losses. The response from Blaenau Ffestiniog still harked back to the old ambition of through lines rather than branch lines in the region. The local MP outlined the history in the Commons and noted:

> Blaenau Ffestiniog [the largest underground slate mining area in Europe] became the hub of a railway system, one part of which [the FR] has unfortunately been closed. I want to know whether the other two parts will follow suit. We want to see the two railways united to give them a true purpose and function. This is a problem which has economic and social implications. A glance at the map shows that if these two termini were connected a through railway would run all the way from Ruabon to Llandudno Junction on the North Wales coast.
>
> It is claimed that the railways are uneconomic. Even so they are not unique in this respect. What could be expected under the present stupid arrangements? Virtually, we have two culs-de-sac and culs-de-sac never become flourishing thoroughfares. Break down the partition wall between them and they become a thoroughfare with all the possibilities and consequences of a thoroughfare.

The same is true in relation to these railways. If the two railways were linked together the whole picture would change.

The estimated cost of forging this link was £50,000 (£1.1million) according to the MP but in rejecting the plea, the government argued it would be almost a third more than that and would not break even. The minister listed significant technical issues and said there was no prospect of making the connection. As we shall see, it did prove possible to construct a link in support of different priorities.

During the debate on modernisation in February 1955, the government made clear its intentions in the Commons. 'The enormous nineteenth century network of railways in this country must be reduced. A start has been made by the Commission ... Uneconomic branch lines have been closed, but the process must go a good deal further.' True to its word, the original VCR closed in September 1955 soon after the conclusion of a long national rail strike, and hard on the heels of the closure of the short branch to Holywell Town a year earlier. This time there was a reaction by the North Wales Development Council. It noted that there had been a firm but unsuccessful attempt to block the closure of the short Holywell

At Trefnant there is a reasonable number and mix of passengers on the platform as the local train for Rhyl approaches in the final year of passenger operation of the original VCR in 1955. **(WRRC)**

Rioters captured Hope station in 1863 but it survived almost another century before closure. Here, it nears the end of its services to passengers with staff gathered for a picture, perhaps for the last time. **(LNWR Society)**

branch and wanted a similar stance on future closures. It wanted the Transport Commission to state its longer-term policy for north Wales and considered that:

> In a nationalised undertaking profit should not be the main consideration, but service, particularly in rural areas… small branch lines all over North Wales had been closed without any regard for the comfort of the people … the prospect for rural area of Wales was … bleak [the question was] 'Where is it going to stop?'

For the rest of the 1950s only three more stations closed, Padeswood and Buckley and Hope Exchange in 1958 and an end to the saga of Treborth station when legislation finally allowed closure in 1959, a little over 100 years after the first

There were high hopes for the introduction of DMUs on branch lines in north Wales, for example to Blaenau Ffestiniog from March 1956. The is no evidence of success in this picture taken at Llandudno Junction at the height of the tourist season in August 1959. **(Online Transport Archive)**

attempt. There was an effort to improve services and reduce cost by the increased use of DMUs on the lines to Amlwch and Blaenau Ffestiniog from March 1956. But it was too late.

The pressure on branch lines continued into the 1960s. Contributors to a debate on the rural depopulation and unemployment in Wales in 1961 made a strong connection with the closure of branch lines, an issue also raised at an early meeting of the new Welsh Grand Committee when it debated the closure of the Bala to Blaenau Ffestiniog line in 1960. That closure put paid to any idea of a through line from the north coast to the Midlands. The creation of Llyn Celyn to supply Liverpool hastened the closure, with water flooding the former GWR line. It was a defining moment in the quest for a more independent Wales leading to the enduring nationalist cry of '*Cofiwch Dryweryn*' (Remember Tryweryn).

Denbigh MP William Morgan saw this as the start of a further assault on Welsh branch railways and said so in the Commons on 14 April 1961:

Dolwyddelan is quiet in August 1959, and steam clearly still had a role to play on this branch. **(Online Transport Archive)**

A balance has to be kept by BR between economic efficiency on the one hand and the service of the public on the other. There is, however, serious concern in North Wales about the threatened further closure of branch lines there. A good deal was said in the Welsh Grand Committee … about the closure of the Bala and Blaenau Ffestiniog line. … I think that I can put up a stronger case about the proposed closure of the Ruthin—Denbigh—Chester line, which is the last link between the more highly populated areas of Denbigh and Ruthin and the surrounding countryside and the main line. The only other link to Rhyl disappeared some years ago.

I understand that an undertaking was then given that this remaining link would remain untouched, but it appears that an assault is being prepared on this, the last communication link between those areas and the main line. I take this as an example, but it is an important example, because, apart from the country people who move in and out of these towns, a substantial number of school children and of workers from Denbigh who work in areas further east make use of this line. It will be appreciated that, in the last analysis, the whittling down of communications of this kind can only encourage further migration from these rural areas.

Whatever the undertaking, all the remaining stations closed to passengers between Chester and Corwen on the route through Mold, Denbigh, and Ruthin in April 1962, the most closures on a single day in north Wales up to that point. It created a 'railway desert' in Denbighshire, simultaneously robbing the passenger rail connection from three significant centres of population and public administration as Morgan had explained. The popular Radio Land Cruise which ran in various forms from 1951, and which relied on the branch lines, ended after ten years.

A Class 4MT 75053 and passenger train arrive at Mold in February 1961 with a competing Crosville bus on the bridge. Passenger services ceased – despite reassurances to the contrary – between Chester and Ruthin in April 1962. The locomotive dated from 1957 and BR withdrew it just nine years later. (Online Transport Archive)

All the stations between Corwen and Chester via Denbigh closed by May 1962, and with them the end of initiatives such as the Clwyd Ranger tour pictured here at Corwen, where the station survived 100 years before closure in 1964. (Transport Treasury)

British Railways deployed Diesel Multiple Units to improve the experience of passengers, particularly on branch lines. This smart example is at Llandudno in 1958 on a Bangor service. (Online Transport Archive)

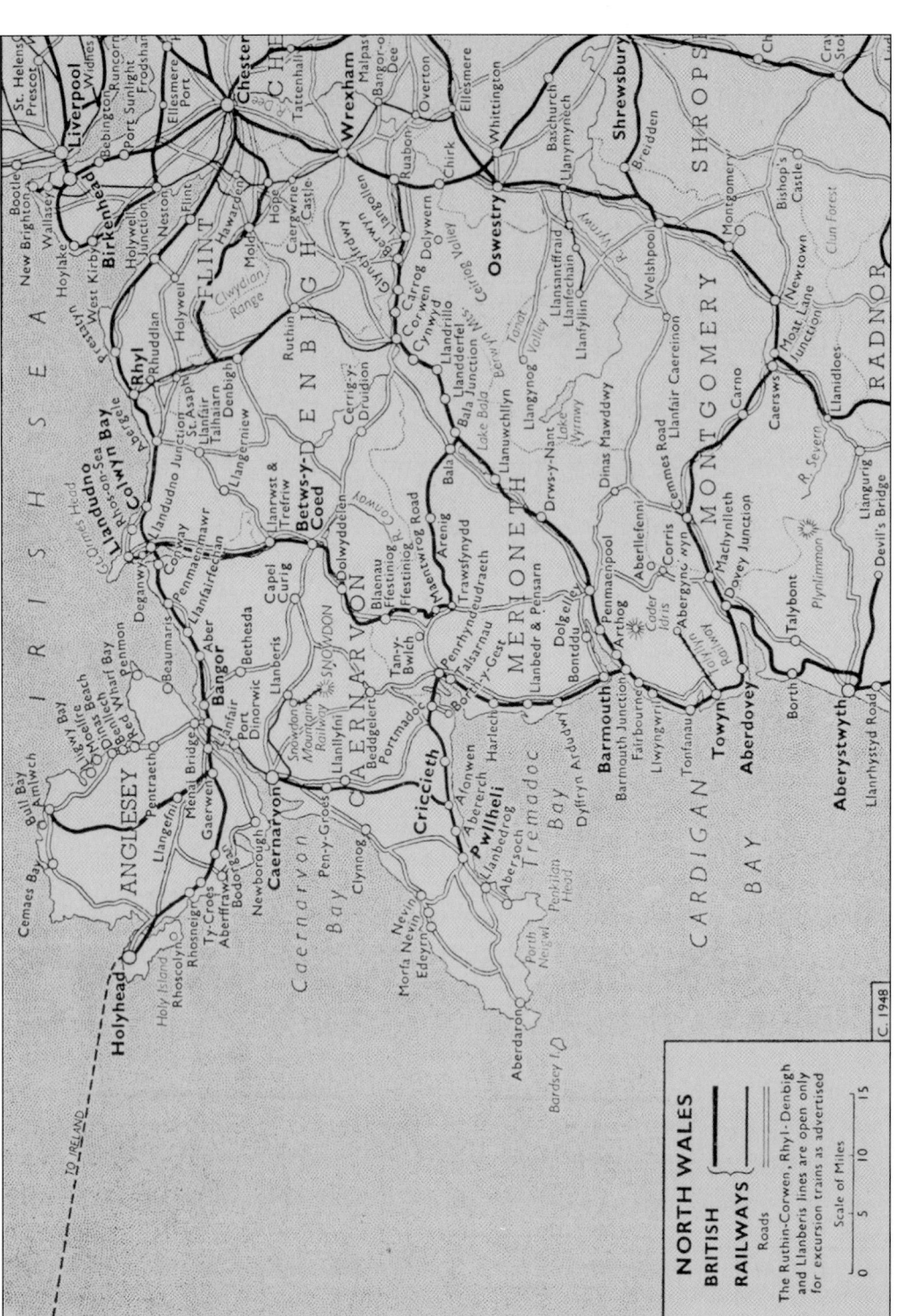

This map shows why the 1956 British Railways Holiday Guide to North Wales referred to parts of the Lleyn Peninsula as 'Wales beyond railways'. Ten years later that description would have applied to most of north Wales away from the coast. (Phil Lloyd Collection)

And so, the saga of branch line closures in north Wales reached 'Beeching', the word which all discussion of rail closures inevitably features. And yet we have seen that by the time of his report in 1963, fifty of the eighty-seven stations on the lines we are considering had already closed – 57 per cent. As Harold Wilson, Leader of the Opposition, pointed out in a debate on 30 April 1963 – exactly one year after the Chester to Ruthin closures – Beeching only did what the government asked him to do:

> Dr Beeching was given a job of surgery to do, and he has done it, deep incisive, antiseptic; amputative surgery on the grand scale, although many railwaymen and railway users ... might prefer the word 'butchery' to 'surgery'. But this was not Dr Beeching's fault. He was told to apply surgery in a situation where surgery was not the main or relevant answer, and ... the surgery has preceded the diagnosis.
>
> The fault lies not in the answer that Dr Beeching has given to the question put to him, but in the question that was put. The fault lies not in Dr Beeching, but in the Minister, in the Cabinet and in the Prime Minister.

In the case of north Wales, the 'deep incisive, antiseptic; amputative surgery' involved proposals to close the remaining branch lines except for the short line to Llandudno – which under Beeching would be the only station of the eighty-seven to survive.

But this time there was a significant reaction. Caernarvonshire MP Goronwy Roberts's speech of June 1964 had the core of the arguments supporting the few surviving branches in north Wales. In opposing the loss of the line from Bangor to Afon Wen, he noted that the line was not a branch but 'part of the railway connecting Caernarvonshire with Liverpool, Merseyside, Chester and Manchester, a region with which we have very close commercial, industrial and, indeed, medical relations'. It was the same point Richard Moon made triumphantly at Caernarfon in 1870. Thus, Roberts revived the historical argument about railways in Wales noting that this line was 'the only connecting line in Wales [and] part of a unique circular rail system which runs right around North Wales. Its closure, therefore, would be a matter not of lopping off an end branch but of fracturing a continuous system which, once broken, might be impossible to restore.'

He articulated, 'The general case against the closure ... hardship to the elderly and infirm who depend on rail transport, the hardship to people who have no cars and live far from bus routes ... and the hardship to families coping with

Above: Menai Bridge station was a vital junction linking north and mid Wales and local politicians opposed closure in June 1964 – all to no avail. It survived for only another six months. **(Transport Treasury)**

Below: By 1975 the fine main station building at Menai Bridge was in an advanced stage of decay. **(Phil Lloyd Collection)**

The junction at Afon Wen seems busy enough in the early 1960s to justify the local MP's unsuccessful objection to its closure. **(Transport Treasury)**

luggage, perambulators, and children.' For him closure would mean, 'an injection of additional traffic into roads which are already seriously congested [and so] it would be the height of folly to scrap the railway line in these circumstances [and] the height of wisdom would be to retain it, to improve it, and to extend its use as much as possible.' He thought there was a special case for Caernarfon as 'the county administrative centre [and] a royal borough where, in due course, the traditional ceremony of the investiture of His Royal Highness the Prince of Wales will take place.'

Above and below: The case for the line from Bangor to Afon Wen included the use made by passengers heading to and from holiday destinations such as Butlins near Pwllheli. These two examples are evidence of an extensive traffic into the 1950s and early 1960s. (Transport Treasury)

As the network shrank, BR spruced up the Caernarfon branch in 1969 for the Investiture of the Prince of Wales. D5077 leads a weed-killing train at the temporary platform by the Ferodo works that was the shortest-lived halt in the region. **(Transport Treasury)**

Roberts was also concerned at the limited basis of the Beeching calculations:

> We are told that the line costs too much. How much does it cost in fact? All over the country people are affronted by the tendentious and selective way in which the Railways Board seeks to prove its losses on these lines … How does the Railways Board count its receipts on lines which it wants to close? Does it include in this case, for instance, a proportion of the fares to the Butlin camp travellers, or a proportion of national and local rover type tickets, or a proportion of receipts for through tickets, or receipts from mail and newspaper traffic and passenger trains, or a proportion of paid travel warrants, or receipts from agencies?

D308 returns from leading the Royal Train in 1969. It was the last hurrah for main line rail travel to Caernarfon which ended in 1970. The locomotive survived until 1980. (Transport Treasury)

Replying to the case, the minister emphasised, albeit disingenuously, that closures had 'nothing to do with the Minister or the Government [the railways] decide in the light of their commercial judgment which railway lines they wish to close'.

In the event, the Caernarfon–Afon Wen line closed a couple of months after Labour came to power in October 1964, along with the branch from Gaerwen to Amlwch. The line from Llandudno to Blaenau Ffestiniog survived and showed where government priorities lay at that time. We saw that in 1954 it was too expensive to connect the GWR and LNWR lines in the latter town but by late 1964 government found money.

But the creation of the link did not deliver the through line from Llandudno to Shrewsbury demanded in 1954 because authorities flooded the old GWR line to meet the needs of Liverpool for water. Government only connected the lines within Blaenau Ffestiniog to serve another external interest, the need for a nuclear power station at Trawsfynydd, which became operational about the same time as the reservoir in 1965. The railway line to Amlwch also continued after its stations closed to serve the bromine extraction plant in the terminal town. Caernarvon had an unexpected reprieve after the BTB closed through fire in May 1970, standing in for Holyhead until 1972. The determination of government to abolish these lines is clear from their rapid dismantling, which usually occurred within a year or so of final closure.

The only comfort for those objecting to the closures was the preservation of the line and all but two of the stations between Llandudno and Blaenau Ffestiniog. This decision preceded the 1964 General Election with consent to close Glan Conway and Dolgarrog. Nonetheless, a sense that its passenger services were on borrowed time continued. Three factors provided mitigation: the continued link with the power station until 1998; the opening of the link with the Ffestiniog Railway in 1982; and the arrival of the Welsh Assembly in 1999. Government-backed improvements helped to secure the line, such as reopening closed stations – Dolgarrog in 1965 and Glan Conwy in 1970 and repairs to the tunnel at Blaenau Ffestiniog after a rock fall in 2019. The Welsh government spent £1 million on Dolgarrog in 2019 after flood damage, only for the water supplier to close the bridge that connects the station to the village. Happily, I noted that the bridge had reopened when I visited in May 2023. A most sensible decision was to rename the inconvenient LNWR Llanrwst station as North Llanrwst and create a station in 1989 closer to the centre of the town.

Aside from the problems with flooding and rock fall there have been few incidents of note on this remaining branch line. The low use of small stations such as Dolgarrog was clear when optimistic thieves broke into the booking office in April 1950 but unsurprisingly found no money. Most significant was another serious collision at Llandudno station in January 1969. Just as in 1925, most of the thirty-one injured were schoolchildren preparing to leave the train when it skidded at low speed. One curious event occurred at Tal-y-Cafn – which has had more than its share of drama – when two men assaulted the person managing the level crossing as he closed the gates after the last train passed on 19 April 2017, the only theory for this incident being that the attackers had left the local pub, just missed the train, and took out their fury on the unfortunate employee.

It would now be politically difficult to close this last fragment of the former extensive north Wales branch system and there is no evidence of any such intention.

That is despite its chronic vulnerability to the weather noted in a debate in Cardiff in February 2020, 'Flood devastation ... has seen the railway seriously damaged [after] £7.5 million of investment has gone into it only recently. But this line is beleaguered by problems with even the mildest rain.' It had experienced similar inundation in 2004, 2005, 2011 and 2015 – and during its entire existence, as noted in earlier chapters. It is particularly vulnerable between Llanrwst and Tal-y-Cafn where extensive 'rock armour' protects it, but its future must be in doubt as climate change tightens its grip. It would be interesting to apply Beeching's methods to the line's current financial position, though thankfully government sees such assessments now as too narrow to be useful.

The branch to Llandudno was never at risk of closure even under Beeching. Its terminus is a pale shadow of its former glory but does not carry the sense of neglect that was clear in photographs from the period from Beeching to the late 1990s. Deganwy is a request stop but the former slate quay now features smart housing that betrays little of its former purpose. At Blaenau Ffestiniog, the central station opened in 1982 making the old LNWR station redundant.

Llanrwst station survived as North Llanrwst and is well-kept in this picture from May 2023. (Phil Lloyd Collection)

Chapter 7

LNWR branch lines in North Wales: An Overview

> The urgent need is to implement an integrated road and rail policy for the whole of Wales.
>
> Commons Debate, 24 November, 1966

The development of branch lines in north Wales was a product of the earlier ferocious battle for the lucrative Irish traffic. The victory of the CHR meant that government backed a main line railway through the region that did not serve the needs of the key towns in the interior north Wales and posed a threat to the shipping interests that plied between the northern coastal towns. As the prominent engineer James Walker noted in 1843, while supporting a line to Porth Dinllaen as a competing line rather than an alternative to the CHR, if the thinly populated and mountainous part of Wales did not get a railway as part of the line towards Dublin, it would be a long time before they benefited from any railway communication. Had the line been built to Porth Dinllaen it is possible to imagine it as the spine of a railway network in north Wales with connections from it to Ruthin, Denbigh, Mold, Rhyl, Llandudno, Blaenau Ffestiniog, Caernarfon and Bangor. That would have gone with the grain of the north Wales economy in 1850 rather than against it.

It was not to be. What north Wales got was a jealously guarded route to Holyhead along the north coast and a series of branch lines, often built or bought specifically to frustrate any attempt to compete with the LNWR. Admittedly, later branches aimed to exploit the growing slate traffic, but they were small-scale operations, aside from the tunnel to Blaenau Ffestiniog. The last branches to Dyserth, Holywell and RWB had the appearance of sops to local feeling as the LNWR learned to appease rather than ignore local opinion in the era of growing democracy.

There is little evidence that the LNWR ever regarded the branch lines as a priority, especially as the CHR became increasingly profitable with the growth of the tourist industry. Locals grumbled about inferior quality rolling stock and engines, timekeeping, and a lack of services outside the high tourist season. By contrast, there were local attempts to develop railways that met the needs of the

Welsh economy. The efforts of Savin, Piercy, Davies, Robertson and latterly Watkin and Gladstone stand out as designed to address local interests rather than those of the metropolis. But it was an unequal struggle against the largest and one of the most powerful industrial corporations in the world.

The case brought by the tiny MDJR against the LNWR in 1914 encapsulated the frustrations with railway provision in rural north Wales. It argued that the LNWR prioritised its main line traffic, invested little in the branches, prevented any local initiative, and took little interest in the needs of the local economy. Once again, the LNWR won the case and the principle that it could do what it liked with its business.

We noticed in the narrative that destroying the Welsh language was sometimes an informal aim for railway developers in rural north Wales. Did they succeed? As early as 1854 the Welsh bard Talhaiarn thought that 'Railways will kill her [the language] at last'. The distinctly metropolitan attitude of the LNWR suggests that it was sympathetic to the idea. By 1899, the Dean of St Asaph could note that 'Schools, railways, daily English newspapers, English residents all combined to further a flowing tide [of Anglicisation]. Let it be so'. But there is a counter argument that the extensive branch network prevented the depopulation of rural Wales and thereby sustained small communities and their language, and the later loss of such branches did more harm. It seems therefore that railways initially damaged but may have later sustained the Welsh language.

The period of LMS operation in north Wales had a different feel from that of the LNWR. It appeared determined to take on the threat from road transport by increasing services, speed, comfort, and infrastructure. It showed greater flexibility and imagination in its efforts to generate new traffic and slowed down the rate of decline in railway receipts in north Wales. Yes, it closed lines, but closures were on a small scale, were difficult to dispute and the LMS replaced them with good alternatives. The Second World War both slowed the immediate decline and furthered the future demise of the railways. It did so by guaranteeing the traffic but exhausting the system so that railways struggled to cope with road competition into the 1950s.

The era of BR control in north Wales is difficult to assess. Like the LMS, it started with small-scale closures up to 1955 and made significant attempts to sustain the traffic. Dieselisation helped and the 150-mile Radio Land Cruises were a notable innovation from 1951. It made effective use of the branch lines in a circular tour of north Wales, proving Piercy's argument from the 1860s that north Wales needed connected railways that served the whole region rather than dead end branches.

The period after the 1955 railway strike saw increased closures. There was a consensus that the railway era was over, and the motor car was the future for passengers. The rail network continued as the effective 'national grid' for coal and mineral distribution so that heavy freight to and from remote places often continued. For passenger traffic, 'Beeching' is the word associated with its demise, but his contribution to the process was to engineer its culmination rather than its start. The drive to 'make the railways pay' according to a narrow balance sheet was unstoppable, and once government gave Beeching that brief the outcome was inevitable. By January 1965, the branch line 'network' had disappeared and all that remained was the thirty-mile fragment from Llandudno to Blaenau Ffestiniog, and (briefly) the line to Caernarfon, around 24 per cent of the total. Once the latter closed to passengers in 1970, after the Investiture of the Prince of Wales, just 18.5 per cent remained.

Accepting, as we should, that closures were inevitable, could the process have left a network that served north Wales better than the current one? The key date here is not 1964 when the Beeching closures took place, but 1962 which saw the end of passenger services, despite assurances to the contrary, on the line from Saltney Ferry to Ruthin. Denbigh MP William Morgan argued strongly that this line was a special case because it was the only rail link between the key administrative towns of Mold, Denbigh, Ruthin and Corwen and larger towns and cities in England and north Wales. Surely any sensible overview of north Wales would see that line as vital, more so than Caernarfon-Afon Wen, Gaerwen-Amlwch and even Llandudno Junction-Blaenau Ffestiniog.

The 1956 BR *Holiday Guide* referred to parts of the Lleyn Peninsula as 'Wales beyond railways', but the scope of that term is now extensive in north Wales.

Estate agents invariably list distances to the nearest railway station on their property particulars, the figures for Mold, Denbigh, Ruthin and Corwen are instructive. And these are 'as the crow flies' distances, not real travel distances. Mold is 3.8 miles from Penyffordd which has no direct service to Chester, Liverpool, or Manchester; Ruthin is 10.8 miles from the same station; Denbigh is 10.2 miles from Rhyl which has a good service, and Corwen is 13.4 miles from Chirk, which is also well-served. If Chester-Corwen remained open there may have been a stronger case to keep the line from Corwen to the Cambrian line, thereby creating links with Bala, Dolgellau, Barmouth and Aberystwyth – the links that Savin, Davies, and Piercy had argued for in the 1860s. If the line from Bangor to Caernarfon had stayed open – a route currently covered by a frequent and crowded bus service – and the line from Bangor to Llangefni survived, then the main administrative towns of north Wales would have had a vital rail link.

It is hard to argue with the conclusion of Gwynfor Evans, Plaid Cymru MP elected in 1966 when he told parliament that year:

> The urgent need is to implement an integrated road and rail policy for the whole of Wales. Up to now they have been dealt with separately, almost in isolation from each other. Not only should road and rail policies be integrated each with the other; they should also be an integrated part of a social and economic policy for the Welsh nation. Regard should be had for the effect of every one activity on every other aspect of Welsh life, which must be considered as a seamless web. Otherwise, the best-intentioned actions may do more harm than good. The transport plan must be part of a Welsh development plan which creates the conditions for balanced growth in our industrial, economic, social, and cultural life. This requires a Welsh transport board.

By then the time had passed to save the rail branch network of north Wales. There have been suggestions that the line to Caernarfon might return, with Llangefni being the other candidate for the return of rail. On this, I identify with Captain Davies, Harbourmaster of Porth Dinllaen in 1896 estimating the chances of a line to that port. 'My hair is grey but it will turn black again before such schemes succeed!'

The story of the LNWR branch lines in north Wales is one of missed opportunities, lack of strategic vision, over-provision, and a chronic lack of coordination. The fact that these lines were 'branches' rather than through lines was the issue. Instead of Chester to Corwen it could have been Chester to Aberystwyth, Llandudno to Blaenau Ffestiniog could have been Llandudno to Shrewsbury, and Bangor to Afon Wen could have been Bangor to Swansea.

And such a system may have helped in a way that has appeared more recently. The threat of climate change is acute and likely to affect the CHR, especially between Chester and Abergele where sea levels have historically threatened the line and are sure to do so in future. If the line from Mold through Bodfari existed, it could extend to the coast at Abergele and replace the sea-threatened stretch of the CHR. That would create the route from Holyhead to London via Mold and Wrexham to Shrewsbury supported by engineer Francis Giles in 1843 – safer from rising water levels.

The modern study of branch railways in north Wales is an exercise in industrial archaeology. The short branches to Holywell, Bethesda and Dyserth have become useful and attractive leisure routes, the lines from Denbigh to Rhyl, Corwen and Mold have disappeared, though some station buildings have survived, as is the case on the Llanberis route. The track bed for a substantial proportion of route from Bangor to Afon Wen is well-used, while the track itself is still in place from

Gaerwen to Amlwch, though long disused and mostly overgrown. The branch to RWB and Benllech is barely visible, except for the distinctive bridges and the attractively preserved main building at Holland Arms.

Let Benjamin Piercy have the last word on north Wales branches as a man who could have created a system more able to resist many of the closures after 1955. While struggling to stop LNWR acquisition of the VCR in 1860 he told a shareholders' meeting:

> He had attended there in the interest of the extension of their railway through the heart of Wales. He was pledged to those extensions over and over again and it was therefore his duty not to give way to his feelings ... He looked upon the [VCR] as a mere link in an important system of railway which he hoped soon to see developed in North Wales.

Sadly, what the LNWR gave north Wales was a series of unconnected branches, doomed to disappear once the pre-eminence of railways passed.

Holland Arms opened in 1865, closed in 1952 and is well-preserved as part of a private dwelling in 2023. This picture is from the A5 with the A55 dwarfing the structure, a symbol of road power in the region. **(Phil Lloyd Collection)**

Above and left: The branch to RWB opened in 1909 and offered timetabled passenger services for only twenty-one years. Traces of the line remain, such as the site of Ceint station (with dotted lines to show where it was) and the distinctive bridge design at Rhyd-y-Saint, both seen here in 2023. (Phil Lloyd Collection)

Right and below: *In contrast to the rest of the Amlwch branch, the track at Llangwyllog seems ready for use in 2023. At Rhosgoch the track has almost disappeared, though the bridge strike notice warns of the risk to trains. On this evidence the danger is low. (Phil Lloyd Collection)*

Above: *The most impressive preservation of the former branch lines for leisure use is the stretch from Bethesda that includes the Coetmor Tunnel and the viaduct over the Afon Ogwen.* (Phil Lloyd Collection)

Left: *This picture is from the start of the possible extension towards Marian Mill and shows the former Dyserth goods shed - the passenger station was behind it. The extension stalled because the LNWR and local interests could not agree on how to pay for a bridge taking the road over the proposed railway at this point.*

Colour Picture Gallery

North of Foryd station was the fiercely contested site of the line to Foryd Pier passing under the CHR where the LNWR ejected construction workers in 1859 and the issue ended in court. In May 2023, a Transport for Wales Class 197 for Llandudno passes the site of the conflict. (Phil Lloyd Collection)

Above: *Eyarth cutting proved a significant obstacle to progress on the DRCR and cost the lives of at least four men. By contrast, in May 2023 it was a peaceful footpath.* (Phil Lloyd collection)

Opposite above: *Holywell Junction saw a major smash in January 1912 when a Holywell branch construction train's brakes failed. 55993 parcels train and locomotive 24063 face no such problems in July 1977, though the latter sustained collision damage in April 1979 and was withdrawn from service.* (John Hobbs)

Opposite below: *The Dyserth branch terminus at Ochr-y-Foel saw a collision with the buffers by a freight train in 1906. In August 1970, D5034 quietly loads up with stone at the same place.* (John Hobbs)

Colour Picture Gallery • 203

Near the northern end of the Dyserth branch, 5MT 45044 makes a strong impression while on freight duty on 22 September 1966. It was one of its last outings as BR withdrew it in October 1966 after thirty-one years of service. (John Hobbs)

Tywyn just north of Llandudno Junction saw a train leave the rails and plunge onto the beach in 1866. A TfW class 150 passes close to the spot in 2020. (Phil Lloyd Collection)

In 1902 a Holyhead express raced into a siding at Maesdu to avoid collision with a freight train. 24282 passes serenely through the area with a train from Manchester in May 1978. (John Hobbs)

Work started on the line to Llanrwst in September 1860 at Maenan Abbey. In May 2023, a TfW Class 197 passes the spot heading north. Note the 'rock armour' added to protect the line from flood damage. (Phil Lloyd Collection)

The north portal of the tunnel into Blaenau Ffestiniog is rather more understated than that at the south, though still showing the date of completion. (WRRC)

Gethin's Viaduct is a notable feature of the Blaenau branch. This is it in June 1979, 100 years after opening. (John Hobbs)

In 1891 a heavily loaded train stalled on the steep gradient at Pont-y-Pant station and arrived two hours late at Blaenau Ffestiniog. This is the station in 2018. (Photo © Nigel Thompson cc-by-sa/2.0)

A DMU close to Roman Bridge station on a beautiful day in May 1966. The station name is now Pont Rufeinig. (RCTS Photo Archive, collection of Michael Mensing)

Harsh winter weather was not a regular feature on the branches but there was a severe blizzard at Llanrwst in 1900. More recently, there is a covering of snow at Blaenau Ffestiniog in January 1977 as 24133 attends to freight duties. (John Hobbs)

This picture shows the straightforward design of Dolgarrog station and the 1916 line from it across the river to the aluminium works, viewed from Cadair Ifan Goch in May 2023. (Phil Lloyd collection)

The Snowdon Mountain Railway started with an accident in April 1896 that involved two trains and one death. Here in June 2016, engine No 2 *Enid* passes the site of the disaster at Clogwyn. (Phil Lloyd Collection)

LNWR Chair Richard Moon boasted the tunnel under Caernarfon completed a circle around Wales in 1870. In 2019 it was a small part of the motor vehicle dominance of the town. (Phil Lloyd Collection)

Post-war optimism about the Welsh Highland Railway breaking the railway monopoly in north Wales was short-lived as it had closed by 1936. Happily, it has returned, and in action here at Rhyd Ddu in July 2017. (Phil Lloyd Collection)

The LMS modernised Llandudno station in 1923. It erected these crowd gates that still carry the company badge. The crowds have gone as a TfW Class 197 prepares to leave for Blaenau Ffestiniog on 22 November 2022. (Phil Lloyd Collection)

Above: *Llandudno was the scene of drama in LMS days with several collisions. The BR contrast could not be greater as the crew chat in the sun before boarding this Manchester-bound train in May 1978.* (John Hobbs)

Below: *This picture of 47482 from Euston at Rhyl in March 1976 shows the dismantling of railways in north Wales, with the station almost halved in size, including the loss of the bay platform that once served the Clwyd branch. A supermarket filled the space to the right, as also happened at Caernarfon and Mold.* (John Hobbs)

Above: *In 1964 Caernarvon became the terminus of the line south from Bangor for the first time since 1870. In a typical post-Beeching scene of decay, a DMU appears to have no passengers in June 1965 – and little further use for Caernarvon's five platforms.* **(Transport Treasury)**

Below: *Blaenau Ffestiniog North Station and its branch were lucky survivors of the Beeching axe. The station looks well-kept in this picture from the early 1960s in contrast to Caernarvon in the earlier picture.* **(Transport Treasury)**

Passenger services have long gone from Amlwch, but the Octel trains continued for a while. 25154 dwarfs the houses and vehicles as it passes through the town in February 1978. (John Hobbs)

There was briefly a thriving business in enthusiast travel on the remaining branches as here at Mold on an appropriately murky day in May 1969 with the Welsh Borderer Tour led by D5075. **(Transport Treasury)**

It was far too expensive to connect the two stations at Blaenau Ffestiniog in 1954 but somehow government found money when the nuclear power station opened eleven years later. In May 1979, a train headed by 25302 threads its way through – a hundred years after the LNWR reached the town. (John Hobbs)

The mobile patrol crew member waits to close the gate after 150282 leaves the well-kept Tal-y-Cafn station in May 2018. In April 2017, two men attacked a staff member undertaking this duty for the last train of the day. (Phil Lloyd Collection)

TfW spent £1 million restoring Dolgarrog after significant flooding only to find that the bridge giving access to the village had closed. Happily, the link was restored as a Class 197 rolls through the deserted request stop in May 2023. (Phil Lloyd Collection)

The new station at Llanrwst meets the needs of the local people rather than the landowners as with the original site. A good crowd joins the train to Llandudno for a May Bank Holiday trip in 2023. (Phil Lloyd Collection)

Above: *Deganwy in March 2022 demonstrates the shift in the role of railways in north Wales. The buildings on the station have gone, there are houses on the old slate quay and mass holiday travel by train is no more. (Phil Lloyd Collection)*

Below: *The new central station at Blaenau Ffestiniog opened in 1982 and is a welcome connection with the Ffestiniog Railway. Here 150282 awaits departure in 2017 with the FR platforms to the right of the picture. (Phil Lloyd Collection)*

Appendix

London and North Western Railway Branch lines in North Wales

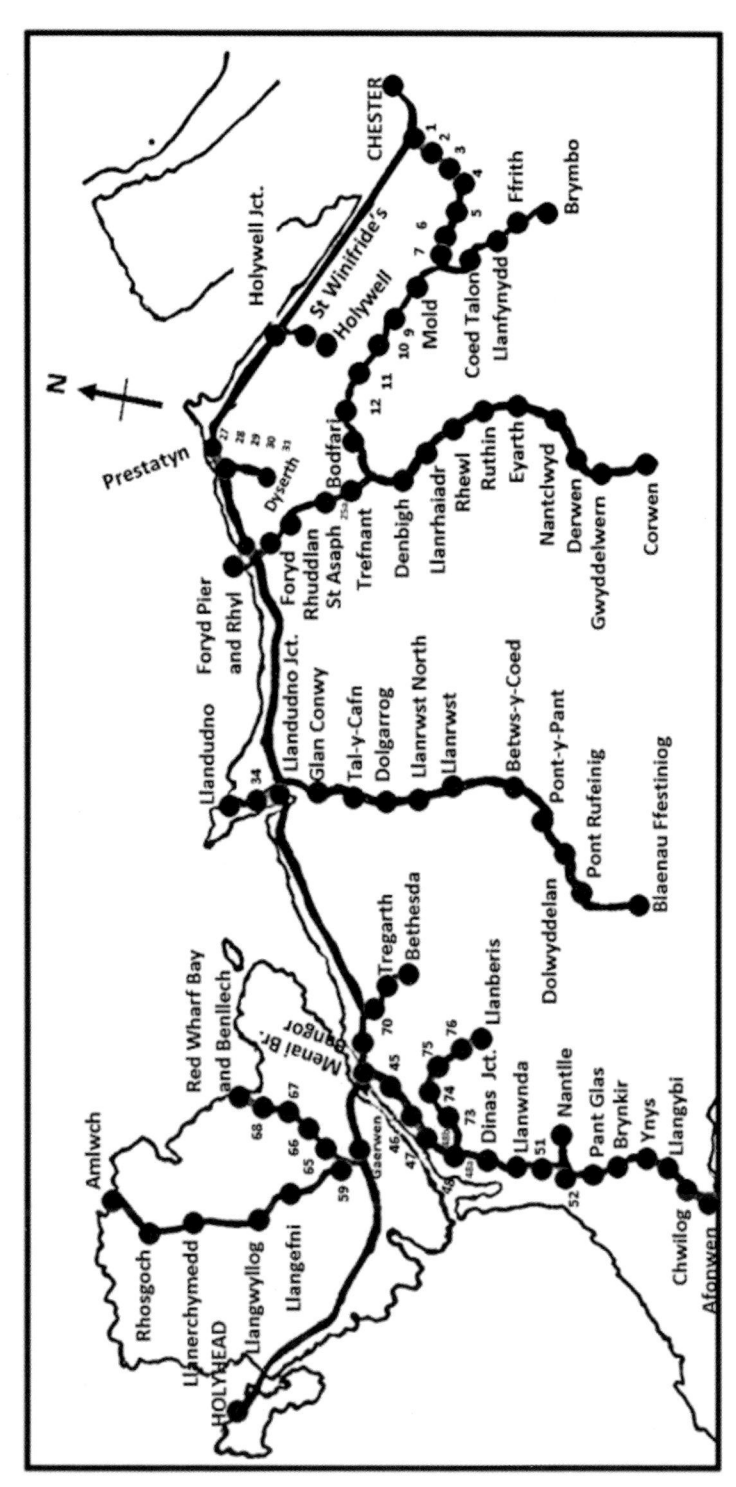

Miles	No.	CHESTER TO DENBIGH	Opened	Closed	Notes
0		Chester	1848		
3.75	1	Saltney Ferry	1891	1962	Fatality 1931
4.75	2	Broughton and Bretton	1849	1962	Gladstone's funeral June 1898
6.25	3	Kinnerton	1891	1962	'Dullest station in the world' 1904
9	4	Hope	1849	1962	Captured by rioters 1863
9.25	5	Hope Exchange	1867	1958	Great Central Railway station
10.75	6	Padeswood and Buckley	1850	1958	Discovery of oil? 1865
11.5	7	Llong	1849	1962	Closed 1917-1919
13.75	8	Mold	1849	1962	Riot at the station 1869
		MOLD TO DENBIGH			
0		Mold			
2.5	9	Rhydymwyn	1869	1962	Death of Sarah Griffiths 1878
3.5	10	Star Crossing	1914	1962	Closed 1917-1919, Derailment 1934
5.75	11	Nannerch	1869	1962	Attempt to derail a train 1906
9.25	12	Caerwys	1869	1962	Brakeman crushed 1875
11.5	13	Bodfari	1869	1962	Tithe riot 1887
15.5	14	Denbigh	1858	1962	Employee crushed 1861
		DENBIGH TO CORWEN			
0		Denbigh			
3.25	15	Llanrhaiadr	1862	1953	Horse injured 1891
5	16	Rhewl	1862	1962	Visit of Lord Napier 1868
7.75	17	Ruthin	1862	1962	A hawker killed on the line 1895
8.5	18	Eyarth	1864	1953	Train derailed by a stone 1865
11.5	19	Nantclwyd	1864	1953	Local aristocrat celebrations 1885
13.5	20	Derwen	1864	1953	Death in the siding 1904
16.25	21	Gwyddelwern	1864	1953	Stalled train causes chaos 1877
18.75	22	Corwen	1864	1964	Dee bridge completed 1863
		RHYL TO DENBIGH			
0		Rhyl	1848		
1	23	Foryd	1858	1885	Line opened to the pier 1864
3.5	24	Rhuddlan	1858	1955	Two horses killed by a train 1882
6	25	St Asaph	1858	1955	Derailment 1860
7	25a	Llannerch Park	1858	1871	Private Halt for VCR director
8.5	26	Trefnant	1858	1955	Troops using this station 1915
11.25		Denbigh			
		PRESTATYN TO DYSERTH			
0		Prestatyn	1848		
0.1	27	Chapel Street	1906	1930	
0.5	28	Woodland Park	1905	1930	Called Rhuddlan Road until 1923
1.25	29	St Melyd Golf Links	1923	1930	
1.75	30	Meliden	1905	1930	Station improvements 1908
2	31	Allt-y-Graig	1928	1930	
2.5	32	Dyserth	1905	1930	Accident 1906

Miles	No.	LLANDUDNO TO LLANDUDNO JCT.	Opened	Closed	Notes
0	33	Llandudno	1858		Accident 1925
2	34	Deganwy	1866		Two sailors killed 1909
3.75		Llandudno Junction	1858		
		LLANDUDNO JCT. TO BL. FFESTINIOG			
0		Llandudno Junction			
1.25	35	Glan Conwy	1863	1964-1970	Stationmaster injured 1900.
5.5	36	Tal-y-Cafn	1863		Accidents 1864, 1904
8.25	37	Dolgarrog	1916	1964-1965	Burglary 1950
11.25	38	North Llanrwst	1863		Death in the station yard 1864
11.75	39	Llanrwst	1989		Opened 1989
15	40	Betws-y-Coed	1868		Death of passenger 1880
19.25	41	Pont-y-Pant	1879		Stalled train 1891
20.75	42	Dolwyddelan	1879		Death on the line 1881
22.5	43	Pont Rufeinig [Roman Bridge]	1879		Site of potential new railway 1896
27.5	44	Blaenau Ffestiniog	1879		Replaced by a central station 1982
		BANGOR TO AFON WEN			
0		Bangor	1848		
1.5		Menai Bridge	1858	1966	
2.5	45	Treborth	1854	1959	Closed briefly during 1858
4.75	46	Port Dinorwic	1852	1960	Station in poor condition 1927
6.75	47	Griffiths' Crossing	1854	1937	Double fatality 1859
8.75	48	Caernarvon	1852	1970	Poor safety record 1873-1907
10.25	48A	Carnarvon Pant	1867	1870	Connecting bus fatality 1868
12	49	Dinas Junction	1877	1951	WHR opens 1923
12.5	50	Llanwnda	1867	1964	Pwllheli Road until 1877
13.75	51	Groeslon	1867	1964	Fatal accident 1886
15.75	52	Penygroes	1867	1964	Stones on the line 1912
19.5	53	Pant Glas	1872	1957	Snow drifts 1928
21.25	54	Brynkir	1867	1964	Multiple fatalities 1866
23.5	55	Ynys	1872	1964	Death of cattle 1875
25	56	Llangybi	1872	1964	Whirlwind destroys signal 1931
26	57	Chwilog	1867	1964	Multiple crash injuries 1872
27.5	58	Afon Wen	1867	1964	Fatality 1936
		GAERWEN TO AMLWCH			
0		Gaerwen	1849	1966	
2.25	59	Holland Arms	1865	1952	Accident 1891
4.5	60	Llangefni	1865	1964	Non-fatal incident 1891
7	61	Llangwyllog	1866	1964	Fatal shunting accident 1894
11	62	Llanerchymedd	1866	1964	Multiple fatalities 1877
14.5	63	Rhosgoch	1867	1964	Hero's welcome 1900
17.5	64	Amlwch	1867	1964	Derailment 1900

Miles	No.	HOLLAND ARMS TO RED WHARF BAY	Opened	Closed	Notes
0		Holland Arms			
1.75	65	Ceint	1908	1930	Visit birthplace of the Tudors 1915
2.75	66	Rhyd y Saint	1908	1930	
4.75	67	Pentraeth	1908	1930	Line destroys historic site 1907
6.25	68	Llanbedr-Goch	1909	1930	Drunken passenger arrested 1910
6.75	69	Red Wharf Bay and Benllech	1909	1930	Traeth Coch is "Red Wharf" in 1909
		BANGOR TO BETHESDA			
0		Bangor			
2.5	70	Felin Hen	1884	1951	Fight over slate strike 1904
3	71	Tregarth	1884	1951	Ballast train derailed 1884
4.25	72	Bethesda	1884	1951	Station wrecked in a riot 1902
		CAERNARVON TO LLANBERIS			
0		Caernarvon			
.75	48B	Carnarvon Morfa	1869	1870	Fatality 1869
3.5	73	Pont Rug	1880	1930	Closed 1917-1919, Derailment 1888
5.75	74	Pontrhythallt	1869	1930	Extensive track damage 1869
6.25	75	Cwm-y-Glo	1869	1930	Explosion 1869
9	76	Padarn Halt	1936	1939	Services advertised 1938
9.25	77	Llanberis	1869	1930	Cutting of the first sod 1864
		PENYGROES TO NANTLLE			
0		Penygroes			
1.5	78	Nantlle	1872	1932	Shed lost 1899, Closed 1917-1919
		MOLD TO BRYMBO			
0		Mold			
4.5	79	Coed Talon	1892	1950	Farm removal by train 1937
6	80	Llanfynydd	1898	1950	Destruction of station by fire 1947
7	81	Ffrith	1898	1950	Survival of a man hit by a train 1906
8.5	82	Brymbo	1882	1950	GWR station
		HOLYWELL JCT TO HOLYWELL TOWN			
0		Holywell Junction	1848	1966	Construction train crash 1912
1.25	83	St Winifride's	1912	1954	Mass pilgrimage by train 1913
1.75	84	Holywell Town	1912	1954	Train hits the buffers 1925

Bibliography

Baughan, Peter, *A Regional History of the Railways of Great Britain, Volume 11 North and Mid Wales*. Newton Abbot: David & Charles, 1980.

Baughan, Peter, *The Chester & Holyhead Railway: Volume 1 The Main line up to 1880.* Newton Abbot: David and Charles, 1972.

Borrow, George, *Wild Wales*, Project Gutenberg eBook #37665, 2011.

British Railways Board, *The Reshaping of British Railways*, HMSO, London, 1963.

Dodd, A. H. *The Industrial Revolution in North Wales*. Cardiff: University of Wales Press, 1951.

Dunn, John Maxwell. *The Chester & Holyhead Railway*. South Godstone, Surrey: Oakwood Press, 1948.

Ellis-Williams, M, *Packet to Ireland*, Caernarfon, Gwynedd Archives Service, 1984.

France, Richard, *Lord Redesdale and the New Railways,* London 1867.

Lloyd, Philip, *The Chester and Holyhead Railway and its political impact on North Wales and British policy towards Ireland, 1835-1900,* Unpublished PhD thesis, University of York, 2017. http://etheses.whiterose.ac.uk/19201/

Lloyd, Philip, 'The Great Railway Problem': Politics, Railways and Nationalism in North Wales, 1870–1900", *Welsh History Review*, Volume 29, Number 1, June 2018,

Lloyd, Philip, *The Chester and Holyhead Railway: A New History,* Pen and Sword, 2021.

Parry, Edward, *The Railway Companion from Chester to Holyhead,* Chester, Thomas Catherall,1848.

Quick, Michael, *Railway passenger station in Great Britain: a Chronology*. Electronic version, https://rchs.org.uk/railway-passenger-stations-in-great-britain-a-chronology/

Rear, Bill, *From Chester to Holyhead: The Branch Lines*, Oxford Publishing, 2003.

Reed, M. C, *The London & North Western Railway; A History*. Penryn: Atlantic Transport, 1996.

Rolt, L. T. C. *George and Robert Stephenson; The Railway Revolution*. London: Penguin, 1988.

Rolt, L. T. C. *Red for Danger,* London: Pan Books, 1966.

Sharpe, Edmund, *Letter on Branch Railways addressed to Lord Stanley of Alderley*, London 1857.

Simmons, Jack, and Gordon Biddle. *The Oxford Companion to British Railway History from 1603 to the 1990s*. Oxford: Oxford University Press, 1997.

Smiles, Samuel, *The Lives of George Stephenson and of his son Robert*, Harper, New York, 1868.

Steele, Wilfred L., *The History of the London and North Western Railway*, London: Railway and Travel Monthly, 1914.

Vignoles, Keith H. *Charles Blacker Vignoles; Romantic Engineer*. Cambridge: Cambridge University Press, 1982.

Williams, G. Haulfryn. *Rheilffyrdd Yng Ngwynedd. Railways in Gwynedd,* Caernarfon: Gwynedd Archives Service, 1979.

Newspapers

Aberystwyth Observer
Aberystwyth Times
Beehive
Birmingham Daily Post
Birmingham Gazette
Bradford Observer
Cambrian News
Carnarvon and Denbigh Herald
Catholic Times
Central Glamorgan Gazette
Cheshire Observer
Chester Chronicle
Chester Courant
Clitheroe Advertiser
Daily News
Daily Post
Denbighshire Free Press
Derry Journal
Dublin Evening Mail
Eddowes's Shrewsbury Journal
Edinburgh Evening News,
Evening Express
Fife Herald
Flintshire County Herald
Flintshire Observer
Freeman's Journal
Glasgow Herald
Herapath's Railway Journal
Kentish Independent
Lancashire Evening Post
Lancaster Gazette,

Langport and Somerton Herald
Liverpool Daily Post
Liverpool Evening Express
Liverpool Journal of Commerce
Liverpool Mercury
Liverpool Weekly Courier
Llandudno Advertiser
Llangollen Advertiser
London Evening Standard
Ludlow Advertiser
Morning Advertiser
Morning Chronicle
Morning Herald,
Morning Post
North Wales Chronicle
North Wales Express
North Wales Times
North Wales Weekly News
Northampton Mercury,
Prestatyn Weekly
Railway News
Railway Times
Rhyl Advertiser
Rhyl Journal
Rhyl Record
Sheffield Independent,
Shields Daily News
Shipping and Mercantile Gazette
Sunday Gazette
The Free Press
The Times

Welsh Coast Pioneer
Western Mail,
Wolverhampton Chronicle
Wrexham Advertiser

Wrexham Guardian
Yorkshire Gazette
Yorkshire Post

Index

Pages in bold have a subject picture.

Afon Wen 124, 173, **187**
   Fatality 1936, 170
Allt-y-Graig 163
Amalgamation of railways 4
   Welsh amalgamation 42-3, 61, 72, 120, 125
   Creation of LNWR 13, 15
Amlwch 145-146, **148**, 149, **153**, 180, 191, 197, **213**
   Derailment 1900, 150
Anglesey Central Railway 146, 149, 159
Archer, Henry
   And the North Wales Railway 19-21
Ashbury, James 43, 45
Assheton-Smith of Vaynol 104, 113-114, 129

Bancroft, James, 35, 43, 126
Bangor 106, 108, 109, 111, 115, 128-129, 149, 163, 193
Bangor and Bethesda Railway (BBR) 105
Bangor and Caernarfon rivalry 129-130
Bangor and Carnarvon Railway (BCR) 114-116, 130
Bangor and Llanberis Direct Railway (BLDR) 128-130
Beeching, Richard 160, 185, 189
   Closures 195

Bethesda 101-5, **108**
   Riot 1902, 108
Betws-y-Coed 12, 38, 74, 88, 91-**93**, 163
   Fatality 1880 96, 98
Birkenhead 12, 14-16, 23, 34, 74
Blaenau Ffestiniog 82, 89, 92, 94, **97**, **99**, 177, 180, 191-6, **208**, **212**, **214**
   Central station opened 1982 **216**
   Tunnel **95**, **206**
Board of Trade inspections 98, 125, 138, 149
Bodfari 45, 60
   Riot 1887 **62**
Branch line policy, 11-12, 21, 27, 71-72, 76, 84, 161, 163, 172, 185
   Spoiler lines 16, 38
Britannia Tubular Bridge (BTB) 14, 21, 111, 113, 145, 191
British Railways (BR) 175, 181, 194
   Land cruise 182, 194
Broughton and Bretton 16, **17**
   Gladstone's funeral 1898 74
Bridges
   Dee (at Corwen) **40**-41
   Gethin's viaduct 95-96, **206**
   Ogwen viaduct 106
   Shotton (Hawarden) **79**
Brymbo 28, 175

Brynkir **125**, 163
  Multiple fatalities 1866 124
Bulkeley, Sir Richard 148-149
Burnell, George 26
Buses and road competition **20**, 76, 80, 82, 126, 162, 165, **182**, 185, 195

Caernarfon 126, 128, 130, 132, 134, **135**, **146**, 168, **188**, **209**, **212**
  Accident records 138-140
  Investiture 144 (1911), 187 (1969), **189-190**, 196
Caerwys 45, **67**, 71-72
  Brakeman injured 1875, 63
Carnarvon and Bethesda Railway 104-105
Carnarvon and Llanberis Railway 126-134
Carnarvon Morfa station 126, 139
  Fatality 1869 **132**
Carnarvon Pant station 124, 126, **127**
  Omnibus fatality 1868, 126
Carnarvonshire Railway (CR)120, 121, 125, 126, 128, 134
Ceint station 155, 159, **198**
Cerrig -y-Drudion 74, 79-80,
Chapel Street station 78
Chester 13, 15, 26, 41-42, 73, 81
Chester and Birkenhead Railway (CBR) 14-15, 34
Chester and Holyhead Railway (CHR) 6, 10-12, 14, 16, 19, 27-28, 30-31, **37**, 82
Chwilog, 124
  Serious collision 1872, 140, **141**
Civil disturbances and the railways, 61, 62
Coed Talon station, **169**, 175
  Farm removal 1937, 168

Conway and Llanrwst Railway, 11-12, 88-89
Corwen 28, 31, 38-42, 51, 53, 58, 175, 182-**183**
Crosville Motors, 165, **182**
Cwm-y-Glo 131-132, **134**
  Explosion 1869, 132
Davies, David 22, 28, 44
Deganwy **86**, 89, 96, 111, 155, 172, 192, **216**
  Double fatality 1909, 86
Denbigh 23, 25-30, 34, 41-44, 48, **51-52**, 53, 55, 63-64, 67, 155, 163, 181-182
  Fatality 1861, 50
  Railway strike 1911, 80
Denbigh Ruthin and Corwen Railway (DRCR), 31, 41
  Construction, 39, 51
  Phases of ownership, 42-43, 45-47
  Reliability and management, 52-53

Derwen 54-**55**
  Fatality 1904, 57
Dinas Junction **137**-138, 175
  Opening of WHR 1923, 160
Dolgarrog 101-**102**, 168, **208**, **215**
  Burglary 1950, 191
  Flooding, 170, 191
Dolwyddelan station 95, **181**
  Fatality 1881 98
  Name change 95
Drunkenness and the railways 50, 57, 63, 86, 97, 155, 172
Dyserth 78, 163, **200**, **203**
  Collision 1906, 78

Earle, Hardman 90
Education Commissioners 1847 18-19

Index • 227

Eisteddfod 41, 49, 73, 89, 92, 98, 140, 149
Explosives 94, 107, 132
Extreme Weather events 48, 100, 107, 138-139, 149, 170-171, 173,
Eyarth 75, **176**, **202**
    Construction issues 40-41, 51
    Derailment 1865, 52
    Fatality 1952, 175

Failed railway projects
    Cerrig y Drudion 79-80
    Marian Mill 78, **200**
    Porth Dinllaen 39, 121-122
Farming 92, 168, **173**
Felin Hen 106-107
    Disturbance 1904, 108-**109**
Ferodo Investiture Halt **189**
Festiniog Railway (FR) 111, 120, 177, **216**
Ffrith **68**
    Injury of employee 1906 67
Foryd Pier **31-32**, 33-**35**, **201**
Foryd **31-36**
Foryd Junction **37**
France, Richard 43-44

Gaerwen147, 153, 190, 197
Gardner, Robert 33-34, 81
Gauge Commission 1845 23
George's Harbour Railway 82
Gladstone, Sir John 45
Gladstone, William 72, 81
    Attitude to the LNWR 73
    Funeral 74
Glan Conwy 89, 99, **100**, 191
    Severe injury to stationmaster 1900, 98

Glyn, George Carr 15-16, 91
Grand Junction Railway (GJR) 13-15,
Great Western Railway (GWR) 10, 12-13, 15-17, 23, 26, 28, 30-32, 34, 37-39, 41-42 46-47, 54, 73, 81-82, 89-90, 92, 94, 96, 104, 120, 154, 161, 180, 190
Griffith's Crossing 115, **118**
    Double fatality 1859, 116
Groeslon 124
    Fatality 1886, **119**
Gwyddelwern 41, **56**, 58
    Stalled train 1877, 54

Holland Arms **151**, 154, 165, 175, **197**
    Accident 1891, 149
Holywell Junction 163
    Accident 1912, **203**
Holywell Town **77**
Hope and Penyffordd 16, **179**
    Captured by rioters 1863, 65
Hope Exchange 179

Irish Railway Commission 11

Kinnerton 16, **65**
    'Dullest station in the world', 1904, 64

Landowner power 11, 26-27, 37, 41, 79, 89, 115, 120, 129, 134, 146, 152, 154
Legal proceedings 31, 50, 52, 58, 60, 61, 64, 68, 72, 80, 91, 107, 109, 115, 121, 141, 155, 172
Light Railways 75, 152, 154, 160
Liverpool 13-14, 23, 31, 73, 162, 180, 185
Liverpool and Manchester Railway (LMR) 45, 90

Llanbedr-Goch station, **156**
  Passengers molested 1910, 155
Llanberis 128-132, **165**
  Connection to the Snowdon
    Mountain Railway 144
  Cutting of the first sod 1864 143
Llandudno 82-90, **84**, **85**, 153, 155,
  163, 170, 172, 175, **183**, 185, 191,
  210, **211**
  Multiple injuries in collision 1925 169
Llandudno Junction 75, 82, **101**, 163,
  169, **180**, **204**
  Strikes 88, 100
Llanerchymedd 150-**151**, 171
  Multiple fatalities 1877, 149
Llanfynydd **176**
  Fire 1947, 175
Llangefni 145, 147, **152**, 163, 196
  Accident 1891, 150
Llangollen 30, 38-39
  Strategic importance, 26, 37
Llangwyllog 149, **199**
  Fatality 1894, 150
Llangybi 135, 140
  Freak weather event 1931, **136**, 171
Llannerch Park 29
Llanrhaiadr 41, **57**
  Injury to a horse 1891, 55
Llanrwst 11, 88-90, 92, 99, 163, 191, **215**
  Fatality 91,
Llanwnda 115, **117**, 124
Llong 16, 170-**171**
  Closed 1917-1919, 145, 160
London and Birmingham Railway
  (LBR) 14-15
London Midland and Scottish
  Railway (LMS) 72, 161-6, 168,
  172-173, 194

London and North Western Railway
  (LNWR)
  Attitude to branch line development
    and operation 12, 16, 21, 27,
    32-33, 39, 50, 70-71, 74, 76, 84,
    90, 92, 126, 131, 197
  Attitude to the Welsh language and
    culture 61
  Creation 10, 13
  Employee relations 81
  Manipulation 42-44, 126
  Monopoly 15, 21-22, 161
  Power of 45, 67-68, 89, 96, 103-105,
    120-122, 129, 154

Maenan Abbey 89, **205**
Mainwaring, Townshend 28, 32, 34-35,
  52, 79
Maesdu 86, **205**
Manchester 14, 33, 43, 89, 124, 158,
  162, 185
Meliden station 78, 167
Menai Bridge 115, **186**
Military connections 72, 81, 145,
Mining and Quarrying operations 29,
  70, 78, 96, 135, 195
Modernisation 21, 175, 178
Mold 11, 16-18, **20**, 23, 34, 43,
  60-61, 75, 155, 163, **182**,
  195, **213**
  Bus service, 80
  Fatality at the station, 63
Mold and Denbigh Junction Railway
  (MDJR) 41-45, 60-63, 70-74
Mold Junction 16, 74, 111, 169
Mold Railway 16, **18**, 27
Moon, (Sir) Richard 46, 96-97, 105,
  134, 143, 159, 185

Motive power
   Diesel Locomotive, **113**, **118**, **150**, **189**-**190**, **203**, **205**, **208**, **211**, **213**-**214**
   Diesel Multiple Units, **99**, 175, **180**, **183**, **207**, **212**
   Motor trains, **75**, **77**, 78, 88, 155, 166-**167**, 170
   Steam engine, **40**, 48, 54, 74, **97**-**98**, **108**, 124, 131, **148**, **169**, **182**, **204**, **209**-**210**

Nannerch 45
   Attempt to derail a train 1906 **63**-**64**, 70
Nantclwyd 41
   Celebrations for local aristocrat 1885, 59-**60**, 163
Nantlle Railway (NR) 111, 120-122, 124-125, 128
Nantlle 128, 135-**136**
   Shed demolished by a train 1899, 135, 160, 165, 171
Nationalisation 173, 175
North Llanrwst station **192**
North Wales Mineral Railway 15, 19
North Wales Narrow Gauge Railway **137**-138
North Wales Railway (NWR)19-20, 111, 113

Overend Gurney banking crisis 12, 42, 125

Padarn Halt 165-166, 168
Padeswood and Buckley 42, **66**, 179
   Bogus oil discovery 1865, 64

Pant Glas 124, **177**
   Snow drifts 1928, 171
Parliamentary proceedings 10, 13, 21, 28, 34, 42, 44-45, 80, 92, 113-114, 119, 130, 165, 177-178, 180, 196
Pennant, Philip 70
Penrhyn/Pennant 103, 128
Pentraeth 153-**156**, 159
   Destruction of historic site during construction
Penygroes **123**-124, 135
   Stones placed on the line 1912, 141, 163
Peto, Sir Samuel Morton 27-28
Piercy, Benjamin 22, 28, 33-35, 39, 72-73, 121-122, 146, 194, 197
Pont Rug 132, 145, 160
   Derailment 1888, 139
Pontrhythallt **133**
   Extensive track damage 1869, 132
Pont-y-Pant 95, 163
   Stalled train 1891, **207**
Port Dinorwic 113-**114**, 119
   Poor condition of the station reported in 1927 168
Porth Dinllaen 12-13, 19-21, 38-39, 74, 111, 120-122, 124
Prestatyn **75**, 78, 166-167
Preston, Richard LNWR Solicitor 22, 28, 35, 121, 146

Railway Gauge 12-13, 23, 88, 92, 103-105, **106**, **137**-138
Railway impact on animals 50, 53, 55, 92, 119, 141, 168
Railway War 28, 39, 45,

Red Wharf Bay (RWB) and Benllech 153-155, **157-158**, 193, 197
  Objection to Anglicisation of local name 155
Redesdale Lord, 44
Religion and railways 62, 76, 8, 152
Rhewl 41, 54
  Visit of Lord Napier in 1868, 58-**59**
Rhosgoch 149-150, **199**
  Boer War hero returns 1900, 152
Rhuddlan **29**, 48
  Two horses killed on the line 1882, 51
Rhyd-y- Saint 155, **198**
Rhydymwyn 45, 63, **66**, 159, 172
  Fatality 1878, 65
Rhyl 11, 23, 26-29, 31-32, 39, 48, 81, 163, 193, **211**
Road competition 28, 88, 155, 160-165, 168, 173, 175
Robertson, Henry 22, 28, 37-38, 72, 80, 194
Roman Bridge 95, 97-98, 163, **207**
  Site of possible new railway 1896, 74
Ruabon 23, 25, 27-28, 30, 37, 120, 177
Rural development/depopulation 44, 51, 80, 177, 179-180, 182, 194
Ruthin 11, 23-26, 30, 37, 39, 41, **46**, 51, 53-54, 58-59, 71, 79-80, 159, 163, 181-182, 195
  Fatality 1895, 59

St Asaph 27, 29
  Derailment 1860 50
  Sunday rail services 48-**49**
St Melyd Golf Halt 163
St Winifride's **76**
Saltney Ferry 16, 74

Fatality 1931 169
Sandbach, Henry Robertson 88, 90
Savin, Thomas 22, 28, 30-31, 33-35, 42-44, 73, 124-125, 194
Sharpe, Edmund 11-12, 17, 88-91
Ships and Shipping 23, 29, 31, 34, 86, 105, 193
Shrewsbury 12, 15, 19, 23, 196
Shrewsbury and Birmingham Railway 15
Shrewsbury and Chester Railway (SCR) 15, 23, 26, 38
Signalling issues 86, 116, 138, 140, 170-171, 175
Slate 89, 95-96, 101, 105, 111, 114, 120, 128, 161, 177, 193
  Distribution centres 16, 86
  Industrial dispute 107-110
Slavery and north Wales branch railways 45, 88, 90, 103
Smith, Martin 33, 49, 51, 60, 147
  Views on Wales and the Welsh language, 61
Snowdon Mountain Railway **143-144**, **209**
Stalbridge, Lord 78
Star Crossing **71**
  Derailment 1934, 169
Stephenson, George 119
Stones on the line 52, 63, 141, 150
Strikes on the railway 80-81, 88, 100, 178, 195
Sunday observance 48-49, 87

Tal-y-Cafn 88-89, **91**, 92, 99, 191, **214**
  Derailment 1904, 98

Tourism 10, 23, 74, 97, 145, 153, 161
Trawsfynydd 191
Tryddyn Junction **18**
Treborth 113, 115-**116**, 179
Trefnant 29, **178**
    Troops using to access Caerwys camp 1910, 72-**73**
Tregarth 106-**110**, 163
    Derailment 1884, 107
Tunnels
    Blaenau Ffestiniog, 93-96, **95**, 191, 193, **206**
    Caernarfon, 126, 130, 138, 143, 159, **209**
    Coetmor, 107, **200**
    Cwm y Glo, **134**
    Vaynol, 113, 115-116, **118**

Vale of Clwyd Railway (VCR) 26-35, 37, 48-52, 178

Wharncliffe, Lord 21, 126
Watkin, Sir Edward 72-74, 81, 143, 194
Welsh Highland Railway (WHR) 160-161, **210**
Welsh Language 18-19, 21, 61, 91, 155, 194
Whalley, George Hammond 37-38, 120
Women and railways 58, 88, 172
Woodland Park 78
Wrexham 15-16, 19, 23, 25, 27-28, 73-74, 81, 160

Ynys, 135 141-**142**, 170